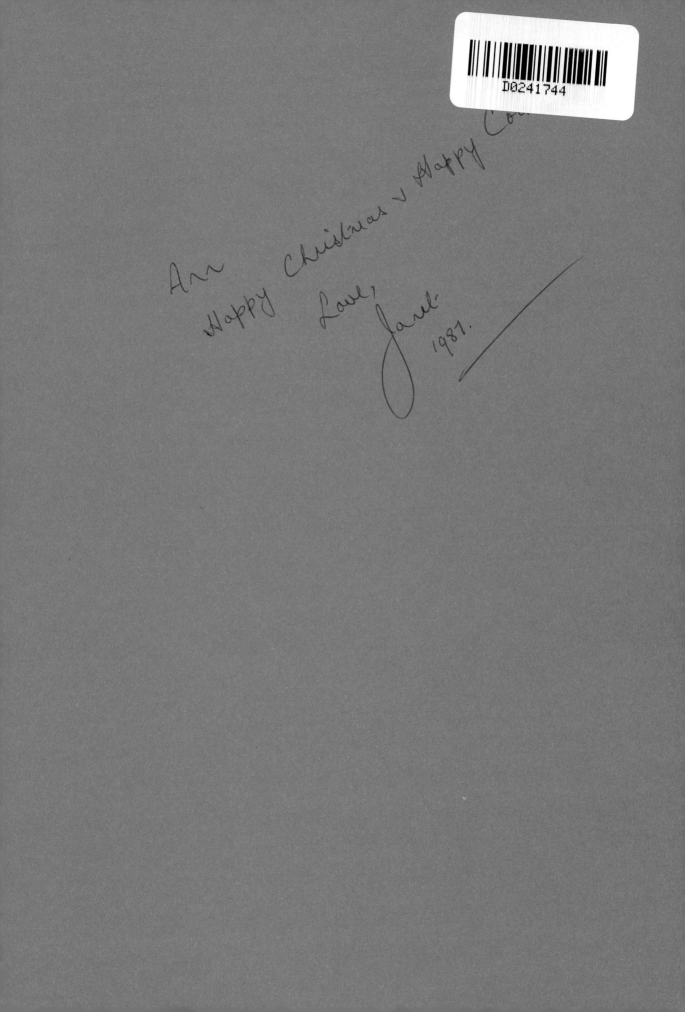

Ann

Happy Christmas ∨ Happy Co[...]

Love,
Jane.
1987.

HIGH-SPEED FOOD

Microwave Meals and Snacks for Young Cooks

Bridget Jones

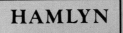

HAMLYN

Photography and Styling by David Burch

Home Economist Nicola Diggins

Designer Jillian Haines

The Author and Publisher would like to thank the following companies for lending ovens to test the recipes: AEG (UK) Limited, Electrolux Limited, Thorn Domestic Appliances (Electrical) Limited and Toshiba (UK) Limited.

Special thanks are due to Sue Staples and Jane Dent from George Abbot School, Guildford, Surrey, and the following pupils who tested and tasted many of the recipes: Stuart Barclay, Sara Britt, Sian Bruton, Julie Channan, David Clark, Sarah Collins, Alexandra Coombes, Melanie Cragg, Rebecca Davis, Mary Duncan, Emma Eastern, Shani Elliot, Joanne Farmer, Vicky Finney, Caroline Golding, Jackie Gravett, Karey Grice, Melanie Hancocks, Livette Henderson, Catherine Jeffrey, Caroline Jessop, Michelle Joyce, Teresa Knapp, Tina Lister, Sorrel Milner, Sally Mitton, Sarah Newton, Lynne Powell, Nicola Reigate, Emily Rumble, Rachel Sakas, Tracey Singer, Amanda Southgate, Lorraine Strudwick and Maxine Wickwar.

Jaqueline Lungley, Katherine Taylor and Anthony Yates from Caterham, Surrey, also helped by testing recipes at home.

The Author and Publisher would like to thank in particular the following for their help and co-operation in providing accessories for photography: Argon of Covent Garden, London; the Covent Garden Kitchen Shop and Strangeways, Covent Garden, London.

First published 1987 by
The Hamlyn Publishing Group Limited
Bridge House, 69 London Road, Twickenham, Middlesex, England

ISBN 0 600 53018 3

Printed in Hong Kong by Mandarin Offset

CONTENTS

INTRODUCTION

What are microwaves?

There are waves all around us – light waves, sound waves and radio waves for example. Microwaves are similar to radio waves, but they are shorter. In scientific terms, they are high-frequency, non-ionising, electromagnetic waves but you do not need to know all that just to cook food in a microwave oven!

What do microwaves do?

Microwaves do not behave in the same way with different types of materials.

The waves cannot pass through metal but they bounce off – just like the sun being reflected off a mirror. However, microwaves go straight through glass and china dishes and they also pass through some plastics. The microwaves are absorbed by some materials. Just like water being absorbed by a sponge, microwaves are absorbed by food.

So, when we put a dish of food in the microwave oven the waves go straight through the dish and are absorbed by the food.

How do microwaves cook food

When the microwaves are absorbed by the food they make the water molecules vibrate at high speed (all foods contain some water). This movement creates a great deal of heat. If you rub your hands together really hard they will feel warm. Similarly, when the water molecules rub together, they produce heat inside the food. It is this heat which cooks the food.

The time it takes to cook depends on the type of food – some foods cook quicker than others.

What else affects the cooking time?

The amount of food you put in the oven makes a difference to the cooking time. The more food there is, then the longer it will take to cook. Small amounts of food cook very quickly.

The shape of the food also affects the way in which it cooks. The microwaves come from the top of the oven, then they bounce off the sides and bottom of the oven so they hit all sides of the food. The waves travel 2.5-5 cm/1-2 in into the food. Neat shapes cook better than uneven lumpy pieces of food.

The way in which the food is arranged is important. Microwaves hit the sides of the dish as well as the top and bottom. So food near the edge of the dish cooks more quickly than food in the middle. Put thick pieces of food round the edge of the dish with thin ends in the middle. For example when you cook chicken drumsticks, put the thick end towards the edge of the dish.

The temperature of the food when it goes into the oven also makes a difference. For example milk from the refrigerator will take longer to heat than milk at room temperature.

The microwave oven

Start by reading the instruction book to the oven. You have to find out how powerful your microwave oven is. All the recipes in this book were tested in 650W ovens.

The amount of waves going into the oven varies – some ovens are more powerful than others. If your oven is more powerful (for example, 700W) or less powerful (600W), then you may have to cook the food for slightly less time or for a little longer.

The waves come into the oven and they are trapped there. They bounce off the walls so that they are all around the food.

Turntables

Some ovens have turntables to move the food between the waves, other ovens have stirrers (like a metal paddle) in the top. The paddles hit the waves and spread them around inside the oven.

Power settings

Each oven has its own power settings. Look at the instruction book to find out what they are and to find out which setting is the most powerful.

Full power (high *or* 100% *or* roast *or* 9 *or* 10)

Medium-high (or bake)

Medium power

Medium-low (or simmer)

Defrost

Hold

Most foods are cooked on *full power* so select the most powerful setting on the oven. *Defrost* setting is used for defrosting food. Sometimes *medium power* is used for cooking certain recipes. In this case use a power setting which is halfway between the most powerful setting and the lowest setting.

Extras

Lots of microwave ovens have extras. You will have fun trying them out and learning to use them but you do not need any extras for cooking the recipes in this book.

Some examples:

Temperature probe – this is stuck into the food and it turns the oven off automatically when the food is hot enough.

Automatic cooking settings – these can sense when the food is cooked and turn the oven off automatically.

Dishes and things to use in the microwave oven

You can use heatproof china dishes in the microwave oven. First make sure that they do not have any metallic trimmings or decorations. Plain china is ideal. Also check that it will stand up to the heat – remember the food is going to get very hot. The hot food touches the plate or dish and this heats the plate.

Ovenproof glassware – like Pyrex – is ideal for the microwave. Basins, mixing bowls, measuring jugs, casseroles and plates made from ovenproof glass are ideal for microwave cooking.

Roasting bags can be used in the microwave and are useful for cooking vegetables. Remember that you must not use the metallic ties which often come with roasting bags.

Absorbent kitchen paper can be used to cover some foods which may spit. Or it can be used to cover bread rolls to absorb any steam which would make them soggy.

Cling film which is produced especially for cooking in the microwave can be used to cover dishes – but you should never use ordinary cling film. Leave a small gap at one side so that steam can escape.

Covering food

Remember that you can always cover some dishes with a plate if you do not have a lid or microwave cling film. When a recipe tells you to cover food you *must* do this. Absorbent kitchen paper can be used to cover some food to prevent splattering.

Baskets can be used to hold bread rolls when they are heated. But do not put baskets in the microwave for too long because they absorb some energy and they begin to cook themselves!

Plastic dishes and containers of all shapes are made especially for microwave cooking. You can use some other plastic containers for heating food – but take care – they may melt!

Following the recipes

You will have lots of fun cooking the recipes in this book – they are all tested to give good results without a lot of fuss. If you want to cook fast and easily, then you will love microwave cooking.

There are just a few things to remember before you start cooking. Stick to these rules and your cooking will always be a success. Don't forget about kitchen safety – keep everywhere clean and tidy.

Read the recipe first to make sure that you have everything you need.

Get all the ingredients and cooking utensils together before you start.

Always measure ingredients properly.

Use either metric or imperial measures – not a mixture of both.

When the recipe says 'tablespoon' or 'teaspoon' always use a proper measuring spoon – not just any big or small spoon from the drawer.

Take particular care when using the microwave

Never use metal containers or leave metal utensils (like spoons) in the microwave.

Make sure you use the proper power setting and that you use the timer properly.

Use oven gloves to lift dishes which have been in the microwave oven for several minutes – they get hot from the food.

When uncovering food which has been cooked in the microwave, protect your hand with a tea-towel and open things away from you because a lot of steam may escape.

Remember – do not use the microwave empty or sparks will fly round inside.

Defrosting food

Use the defrost power setting to defrost food. Sometimes you can use full power if you want to heat the food up as well as defrost it. You can also use full power if the item is small or light, for example bread rolls. Remember these notes when defrosting anything:

Remove any foil wrapping.

Place the food on a plate and cover foods which are in a sauce or which may dry out.

Unless you know exactly how long it will take, give the food a short defrosting time. Check to see how it is getting on. You can put it back if it is still frozen. When ready the food should still feel slightly icy unless you want it to be hot.

When defrosting more than one item put them as far apart as possible on a plate or in the microwave.

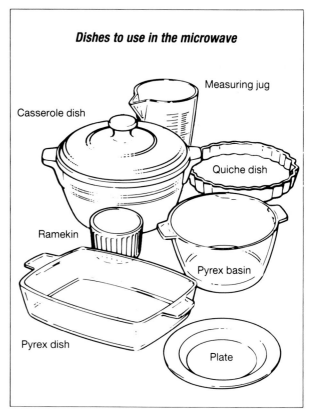

Dishes to use in the microwave

Measuring jug

Casserole dish

Quiche dish

Ramekin

Pyrex basin

Pyrex dish

Plate

A guide to defrosting some foods

Food	Setting	Method
Individual cottage pie	Defrost and full power	Cook on defrost for 8-9 minutes. Change setting to full power. Cook for 5-7 minutes, or until hot.
Steak and kidney pie	Full power	Unwrap, remove all foil. Put the pie on a plate. Cook on full power for about 3 minutes. Stick a fork into the pie to make sure that it is hot through. If not quite ready heat for another 15-30 seconds.
Stew (single portion)	Defrost and full power	Remove any metal or foil. Cook on defrost, in the freezer container, for 2 minutes. Turn out into a basin and cover. Cook on defrost for 7-9 minutes. Break up the stew with a fork. Heat on full power for 3-5 minutes or until hot.
Cornish pasty	Full power	Remove wrappings. Put the pasty on a plate. Cook on full power for 1½-2 minutes.
Slice of quiche	Full power	Remove wrappings. Put the quiche on a plate. Cook on full power for 2 minutes, or until hot.
Hamburger (100 g/4 oz)	Full power	Unwrap. Put the hamburger on a plate. Cover with absorbent kitchen paper. Cook on full power for 3 minutes, or until cooked.
Oven chips 100 g/4 oz 175 g/6 oz	Full power	Put on a plate. Cook on full power for: 2 minutes 3 minutes
Frozen peas or mixed vegetables 50 g/2 oz 100 g/4 oz	Full power	Put in a small basin. Cover with a plate. Cook on full power for: 1½-2 minutes 2-3 minutes

A guide to defrosting some foods

Food	Setting	Method
Cheese or ham sandwich	Defrost	Unwrap. Put a piece of absorbent kitchen paper on a plate. Put the sandwich on the paper and cook on defrost for 1 minute. Leave for 2 minutes.
Bread rolls (unfilled)	Full power	Put the rolls on absorbent kitchen paper on a plate. If more than one, put them as far apart as possible. Defrost on full power for:
1 roll		15-30 seconds
2 rolls		30-45 seconds
3 rolls		1 minute
4 rolls		1-1½ minutes

Reheating food

Food reheats perfectly in the microwave. Remember these points:

Start with the minimum time – you can always cook the food a little longer if it is not hot enough when you first look at it.

If it is a big portion of solid food – for example a cottage pie – heat on medium power to give time for the middle to get hot.

If it is likely to dry up or if it is in a sauce, cover the dish. For example, chilli con carne or potatoes with meat and gravy.

When heating vegetables and meat together, cut the potatoes into chunks and put them near the edge of the dish or plate. Put the meat and gravy in the middle. Other vegetables can go at the side. Cover with an upturned dish or lid.

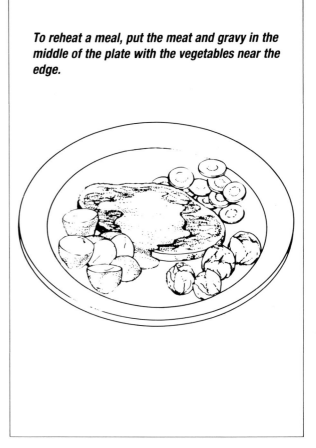

To reheat a meal, put the meat and gravy in the middle of the plate with the vegetables near the edge.

Some useful timings

Food	Setting	Method
Small can of soup (275-g/10-oz can)	Full power	Pour the soup into a dish and heat on full power for 2 minutes. Stir well.
Individual cottage pie	Medium power	Cook on medium power for 7-8 minutes.
Individual steak and kidney pie	Full power	Unwrap and remove all foil. Put the pie on a plate. Heat on full power for about 1½ minutes.
Cornish pasty	Full power	Unwrap and put on plate. Cook on full power for 45-60 seconds.
Slice of quiche	Full power	Unwrap and put on plate. Heat on full power for 45-60 seconds.
Large can of baked beans (425-g/15-oz can)	Full power	Put in a basin, cover with a plate. Heat on full power for 4-5 minutes. Stir well.
Small can (227-g/8-oz)	Full power	As above for 2-2½ minutes.
Spaghetti hoops (small or large)	Full power	As for baked beans.
A meal on a plate – 2 potatoes with vegetables and meat with gravy	Medium	Cover with an upturned dish or use microwave cling film. Heat on medium for 4-5 minutes. Leave to stand 1 minute.
Bolognaise sauce on pasta or spaghetti	Full power	Cover with an unturned plate or microwave cling film. Heat on full power for 4-5 minutes. Leave to stand for 1 minute.
2 cold cooked sausages with 227-g/8-oz can baked beans and 2 scoops mashed potato	Medium power	Cover with an upturned dish or microwave cling film. Heat on medium for 3-4 minutes. Leave to stand 1 minute.

MEATY MAIN MEALS

Home-made Hamburgers

MAKES 4

Ingredients

2 slices bread (about
   50 g/2 oz)
4 tablespoons milk
1 small onion
1 teaspoon dried mixed
   herbs
2 tablespoons tomato
   ketchup
450 g/1 lb minced beef
salt and pepper

To serve

4 burger buns
4 lettuce leaves
2 tomatoes

Cooking dish

flan dish or a large flat plate

Method

1 Cut the crusts off the bread. Break the slices into chunks and put them in a basin. Sprinkle the milk over the bread. Leave for 10 minutes.

2 Meanwhile, peel and grate the onion. Mash the bread with a fork. Add the onion, herbs and ketchup and mix well. Add the minced beef, salt and pepper. Use a wooden spoon to break up the meat. Mix it with the bread until they are thoroughly combined. The mixture should stick together well.

3 Divide the mixture into four. Dampen your hands, then shape a portion of the meat mixture into a flat burger measuring about 10 cm/4 in across. Dampen your hands again and shape the rest of the meat. You will have four burgers.

4 Put the burgers as far apart as possible on a flan dish or large flat plate. Lay a piece of absorbent kitchen paper over the burgers and cook on full power for 5 minutes, or until the burgers are cooked. To see if they are cooked, make a small hole in the middle of one using the point of a knife. If the meat is uncooked it will look red instead of brown.

5 While the burgers are cooking, split the buns in half. Trim the thick stalks off the lettuce leaves. Slice the tomatoes. Place a lettuce leaf on the bottom half of each bun. Put a cooked hamburger on each lettuce leaf. Lay slices of tomato on top of each burger. Put the lid on the bun and serve.

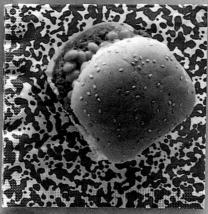

◢ Take Care Cook!

When grating onion take care not to grate your fingers! You may have to throw away a tiny bit of onion but it's better than putting grated fingers in the burgers!

Great Burgers

Try some of the following fillings to make your burgers really special.

Cheese Burgers

Lay a slice of cheese on top of each cooked burger. Cook on full power for about 30 seconds to melt the cheese. Serve in a bun as above.

Bacon Burgers

Before cooking the burgers lay 4 rindless rashers of bacon on a large plate. Cover with absorbent kitchen paper and cook on full power for 2 minutes, or until the bacon is almost cooked. Cook the burgers. Fold a rasher of bacon in half on top of each burger and cook for another 1-2 minutes before putting in the bun. You may like to omit the tomato in this one.

Peanut Burgers

Spread a little crunchy peanut butter over each burger when cooked. Heat for 30 seconds and serve.

Bean Burgers

Put 1 (425-g/15-oz) can baked beans in a basin. Cover and heat on full power for 4-5 minutes. Then cook the burgers. Heat the beans again for 1 minute. Place a burger on each bun and top with baked beans. You do not need lettuce and tomato in this one.

Remember, to go with your burgers, serve relishes like sweetcorn or tomato, pickled onions or gherkins.

Nutty Drumsticks

SERVES 2

Ingredients

2 tablespoons crunchy
  peanut butter
1 tablespoon soy sauce
1 teaspoon lemon juice
1 tablespoon milk
4 chicken drumsticks
sprig of parsley to garnish

Cooking dish

flan dish

Method

1 Mix the peanut butter with the soy sauce, lemon juice and milk in a small basin.

2 Use the point of a knife to cut the skin off the chicken drumsticks. Make three small cuts in each drumstick.

Sausagemeat Surprise

MAKES 8

Ingredients

2 thick slices bread
2 tablespoons milk
75 g/3 oz cheese
225 g/8 oz sausagemeat
salt and pepper
50 g/2 oz sesame seeds

Cooking dish

large plate or flat round dish

Method

1 Cut the crusts off the bread. Break the slices into chunks and put them in a basin. Sprinkle the milk over and leave for 15 minutes. Cut the cheese into eight cubes.

2 Use a wooden spoon to mix the sausagemeat into the bread. Add seasoning and mix well. Divide the mixture into eight portions.

3 Dampen your hands. Take a portion of sausagemeat and press it round a cube of cheese. Roll the meat into a ball to cover all the cheese. Shape the other meatballs in the same way. Keep your hands damp and the sausagemeat will not stick to them. Make sure that there is no cheese showing.

4 Roll the meatballs in the sesame seeds. Put the meatballs in a circle around the edge of a large plate or a flat round dish.

5 Cover with a piece of kitchen paper and cook on full power for about 5 minutes or until the sausagemeat is firm and cooked. Leave for 2 minutes before serving. *The cheese is very hot – so take care or the surprise in the middle may be a burning hot shock!*

3 Place the drumsticks in the flan dish, with the thick ends pointing towards the outside of the dish to make sure they cook well.

4 Use a teaspoon and knife to spread the peanut butter mixture over the drumsticks. Cook on full power for 6-8 minutes. Turn the drumsticks over after 3 minutes and use a spoon to lift the peanut mixture back on top. Make a small cut in one of the drumsticks to make sure they are cooked. If the meat is not quite cooked it will look pink.

5 Place the drumsticks on a plate and garnish with a sprig of parsley.

Chicken Crumble

SERVES 4

Ingredients

2 boneless chicken breasts
100 g/4 oz frozen mixed
  vegetables
1 (290-g/10-oz) can cream of
  chicken soup
salt and pepper
50 g/2 oz mushrooms

Topping

75 g/3 oz fresh breadcrumbs
  (see page 31)
1 small packet crisps
50 g/2 oz cheese
2 tablespoons chopped
  parlsey
salt and pepper
1 small tomato
sprig of parsley to garnish

Cooking dish

casserole dish, large soufflé dish or a round deep dish

Method

1 Use the point of a knife to lift the skin off the chicken at one corner, then pull all the skin off. Cut the chicken into small pieces.

2 Put the chicken in a casserole dish, large soufflé dish or round deep dish. Stir in the mixed vegetables. Pour in the soup and add a little salt and pepper.

3 Wipe the mushrooms with a damp cloth, then cut them into slices. Stir into the chicken mixture.

4 Cover the dish and cook on full power for 5 minutes. Use oven gloves to remove the dish from the oven. Stir the chicken mixture. Cover the dish and cook for another 5 minutes.

5 While the chicken is cooking make the topping. Put the breadcrumbs in a basin. Carefully crush the packet of crisps with your fingers without bursting the bag. Grate the cheese. Mix the crisps, cheese and parsley into the breadcrumbs. Add a little salt and pepper.

6 Sprinkle the topping over the chicken and cook on full power for 3-4 minutes, until hot. Slice the tomato and lay the slices on top of the crumble. Add a sprig of parsley and serve.

Chicken Pockets

SERVES 4

Ingredients

4 slices bread
4 tablespoons milk
4 boneless chicken breasts
1 small onion
1 teaspoon dried sage
salt and pepper
4 rindless rashers bacon
parsley or watercress to
    garnish

Cooking dish

large flan dish

Method

1 Cut the crusts off the bread. Break the slices into chunks and place them in a basin. Sprinkle the milk over the bread and leave it to soak for 15 minutes.

2 Make a slit into each chicken breast so that there is a pocket for the stuffing.

3 Use the point of a knife to separate the skin from the chicken meat at one end of each breast. Hold the corner of the skin and pull it off.

4 Peel and grate the onion. Mash the soaked bread with a fork. Stir in the onion, sage and seasoning.

5 Use a teaspoon to press the stuffing into the pockets in the chicken. Wrap a bacon rasher round each chicken breast to keep the stuffing in. Stick a wooden cocktail stick into the bacon to keep it in place.

6 Place the chicken in a flan dish, putting the thinner ends to the middle of the dish.

7 Cover with a large plate turned upside down, leaving a small gap for the steam to escape.

8 Cook on full power for 8 minutes. Use oven gloves to take the dish from the microwave. Turn the chicken over. Cover the dish and cook for 5-6 minutes, or until the chicken is cooked through. To check that the chicken is cooked, turn one piece upside down and make a small cut into the middle. The chicken should be white, if it looks pink it is not quite ready. Turn the piece of chicken over again to hide the cut.

9 Leave the chicken to stand in the dish for 5 minutes before serving. Garnish with sprigs of parsley or watercress if you like.

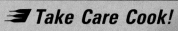 **Take Care Cook!**

Don't use plastic cocktail sticks in the microwave – they melt!

16

Pasta Bolognaise

SERVES 4

Ingredients

225 g/8 oz pasta shapes
about 1.75 litres/3 pints
    boiling water
1 onion
225 g/8 oz carrots
1 green pepper
1 clove garlic, crushed
1 tablespoon oil
450 g/1 lb minced beef
2 tablespoons flour
150 ml/¼ pint water
1 (397-g/14-oz) can chopped
    tomatoes
bay leaf
salt and pepper

Cooking dishes

mixing bowl
casserole dish

Method

1 Put the pasta shapes in a microwave proof mixing bowl and very carefully sprinkle in a little salt. Pour in the boiling water. There should be enough water to cover the pasta by at least 2.3 cm/1 in. Make sure that there is plenty of room in the dish for the water to boil. Cover the bowl and cook on full power for 15 minutes until just soft.

2 Put a colander in the sink. Use oven gloves to lift the bowl from the microwave and strain the pasta in the colander. Give the colander a shake, then tip the pasta back into the bowl and cover.

3 Peel and chop the onion. Peel and slice the carrots. Cut the green pepper in half. Scoop out the seeds and cut off the stalk. Cut the pepper halves into strips, then cut the strips into small pieces.

4 Put the vegetables in a casserole dish with the garlic. Stir in the oil and cover the dish. Cook on full power for 10 minutes.

5 Use a wooden spoon to stir in the meat, breaking it up into small pieces. Mix in the flour, water, tomatoes and bay leaf. Add a little seasoning.

6 Cover the dish and cook on full power for 10 minutes. Use oven gloves to remove the dish from the microwave. Stir well. Cover the dish and cook for another 10 minutes. Leave to stand for 5 minutes.

7 While the sauce is standing put the pasta in the microwave and cook on full power for 2 minutes. Divide the pasta between four plates and spoon the sauce over the top.

Hi-speed Tip

Because spaghetti is so long it is difficult to cook in the microwave. You can break the spaghetti into short pieces and cook it like the pasta.

Curry Meatballs

SERVES 4

Ingredients

1 thick slice of bread
4 tablespoons milk
1 small onion
450 g/1 lb minced beef
1 teaspoon curry powder
salt and pepper
2 tablespoons raisins
25 g/1 oz butter
1 (397-g/14-oz) can chopped tomatoes

Cooking dishes

large plate
large basin or casserole dish

Method

1 Cut the crusts off the bread. Break the middle up into chunks and put them in a mixing bowl. Sprinkle the milk over the bread and set aside for 10 minutes.

2 Peel the onion and cut it in half. Set one half aside to make the sauce. Chop the other half.

3 When the bread has softened mash it with a fork. Mix in the onion, beef, curry powder, a little salt and pepper and the raisins. Use a wooden spoon to break up the mince and to make sure that all the ingredients are well combined.

4 Dampen your hands and take a spoonful of the meat mixture. Press it together well and shape it into a ball about the size of a small egg. The mixture makes 12 meatballs.

5 Put six meatballs in a ring round the edge of a large plate. Cover them with a piece of absorbent kitchen paper and cook on full power for 5 minutes, or until cooked. Cook the other 6 meatballs in the same way.

6 Chop the other half of the onion. Put it in a large basin or casserole dish with the butter and cook on full power for 4 minutes. Add the can of tomatoes and a little salt and pepper. Cook on full power for 5 minutes.

7 Add the meatballs to the sauce, scraping in all the juices off the plates. Mix well and heat for 2 minutes before serving.

◢ Hi-speed Tip

Yellow rice goes well with the meatballs. Put 225 g/ 8 oz long-grain rice in a dish. Add ¼ teaspoon turmeric and a pinch of salt. Pour in 600 ml/1 pint water and cover the dish. Cook on full power for 20 minutes, or until all the water has been absorbed. Cook the rice before you cook the meatballs. Reheat it for 1-2 minutes before serving.

Chilli Con Carne

SERVES 4

Ingredients

1 small onion
1 green pepper
1 tablespoon oil
450 g/1 lb minced beef
2 tablespoons flour
2 tablespoons tomato purée
2 teaspoons chilli powder
1 beef stock cube
450 ml/¾ pint water
salt and pepper
1 (432-g/15.25-oz) can red
   kidney beans

Cooking dish

large casserole dish

Method

1 Peel and chop the onion. Cut the green pepper in half and scoop out all the seeds. Cut off the stalk. Cut the pepper halves into strips, then cut the strips into small pieces.

2 Put the onion and pepper in a casserole dish and add the oil. Stir well. Cover the dish.

3 Cook on full power for 5 minutes. Use oven gloves to lift the dish from the microwave.

4 Add the mince to the onion and pepper. Stir well to break the meat into small pieces. Use a wooden spoon to mix in the flour, tomato purée and chilli powder.

5 Crumble the stock cube into the dish. Pour in the water. Add a little salt and pepper and stir. Cover the dish. Cook on full power for 15 minutes.

6 Open the can of beans and drain off the liquid. Add the beans to the meat and stir. Cook on full power for 10 minutes.

7 Serve the chilli con carne hot with some French bread.

◢ Clever Cook's Tip

Swirl a little soured cream or natural yogurt into bowls of the chilli if you like – it tastes great!

B.B.Q. Spareribs

SERVES 4

Ingredients

1 kg/2 lb meaty pork
  spareribs
1 tablespoon soy sauce
2 tablespoons tomato
  ketchup
1 tablespoon brown sauce
1 tablespoon soft brown
  sugar
2 cloves garlic, crushed

Cooking dish

large casserole dish

Method

1 Lay the spareribs in a casserole dish. Mix all the remaining ingredients in a basin. Brush the sauce mixture all over the spareribs.

2 Cover the dish and cook on full power for 15 minutes. Use oven gloves to remove the dish from the microwave.

3 Use a spoon and fork to rearrange the spareribs, putting the ones from the middle towards the outside. Lift the ones from the edge into the middle of the dish.

4 Cover the dish and cook on full power for a further 10 minutes, or until the spareribs are cooked through. Leave to stand for 2-5 minutes.

◢ Clever Cooks Tip

Make spring onion curls to garnish the spareribs. Wash some spring onions and cut off the roots. Cut off most of the green part. Use a pair of scissors to snip one end of the onions into thin strands. Put the onions into a bowl of cold water and leave for at least 30 minutes. The strips of onion will curl. Dry the spring onion curls on absorbent kitchen paper before you use them.

Pork 'n' Beans

SERVES 4

Ingredients

1 onion
450 g/1 lb minced pork
2 teaspoons dried sage
salt and pepper
1 (397-g/14-oz) can chopped
  tomatoes
1 (425-g/15-oz) can
  barbecued beans or baked
  beans

Cooking dish

casserole dish

Method

1 Peel and chop the onion. Place in a casserole dish. Add the minced pork and break it into small pieces using a wooden spoon. Cover the dish and cook on full power for 5 minutes.

Pork and Apple Kebabs

SERVES 4

Ingredients

225 g/8 oz lean boneless pork
1 orange
1 teaspoon dried thyme
salt and pepper
2 large eating apples
orange slices

Cooking dish

large flan dish
4 wooden skewers

Method

1 Cut the meat into 1-cm/
½-in cubes. Grate the rind
from about half the orange.
Cut the orange in half and
squeeze out the juice. Mix
the orange rind and juice
with the thyme and a little
salt and pepper.

2 Cut the apples into
quarters. Cut out the cores,
then cut each quarter into
3 slices.

3 Thread the cubes of pork
and apple slices on to four
wooden skewers. Lay the
kebabs in a large flan dish
and pour the orange juice
over them.

4 Cover the dish with
microwave cling film or a
plate turned upside down.
Leave a small gap for the
steam to escape. Cook on full
power for about 5 minutes,
or until the meat is cooked.
To check that it is cooked,
stick the point of a knife into
one cube of meat. If it looks
pink and feels soft is is not
quite cooked. It should be
firm but not tough.

5 Spoon the juices over the
kebabs and garnish with
orange slices before serving.

◢ Hi-speed Tip

*Rainbow Rice (see page 22
for the recipe) tastes great
with these kebabs.*

2 Add the sage to the meat.
Sprinkle in a little salt and
pepper. Mix in the chopped
tomatoes. Cover the dish and
cook on full power for
5 minutes.

3 Stir the meat mixture. Add
the beans, mix well and
cover the dish. Cook on full
power for a further 5
minutes, or until the beans
are hot and the meat is
cooked. Serve at once.

Hi-speed Tip

*Try making some hot herb
bread to go with the pork 'n'
beans. Cut eight slices of
French bread. Spread each
slice with butter and
sprinkle some dried herbs
over the top. Put the slices
on a large plate, arranging
them in a ring round the
edge. Cook on full power
for 30 seconds or until
the butter has melted.*

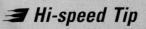

Ranchers

SERVES 4

Ingredients

1 (131-g/5-oz) packet instant
   mashed potato
450 ml/¾ pint water
4 small ham steaks
1 (227-g/8-oz) can baked
   beans

Cooking dishes

large basin
flan dish

Method

1 Put the instant mash in a
large basin and pour in the
water. Stir, then cook on full
power for 4 minutes or until
the mixture looks like proper
mashed potato.

2 Put the ham steaks in a flan
dish. Cover it with a large
plate and cook on full power
for 2 minutes. Turn the ham
steaks over and cover the
dish again. Cook for another
2-3 minutes on full power or
until they are firm, slightly
curled and cooked.

3 If you like, you can pipe the
mashed potato round the
ham steaks. Put a large star
nozzle into a piping bag and
spoon in the potato. Pipe a
high edge of potato on top of
each ham steak. Or instead
of piping the potato, you can
pile up an edge using a
spoon and fork.

4 Put a spoonful of beans in
the middle of the potato.
Cook on full power for 5-6
minutes, or until the beans
and potato are hot.

Rainbow Rice

SERVES 4

Ingredients

225 g/8 oz long-grain rice
1 tablespoon tomato purée
600 ml/1 pint water
½ teaspoon salt
100 g/4 oz frozen peas
100 g/4 oz frozen sweetcorn

Cooking dish

large casserole dish

Method

1 Put the rice in a large casserole dish. Make sure that there is plenty of room for the water to boil. Add the tomato purée and the water. Stir well to dissolve the tomato purée. Add the salt.

2 Cook on full power for 15 minutes. Use oven gloves to lift the dish from the microwave. Add the peas and sweetcorn and cook for a further 5 minutes, or until the water has been absorbed. Fluff up the rice with a fork and serve.

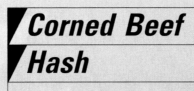

Corned Beef Hash

S E R V E S 4

Ingredients

350 g/12 oz potatoes
1 onion
1 (340-g/12-oz) can corned beef, chilled
salt and pepper

Cooking dishes

large basin or casserole dish
small deep flan dish

Method

1 Peel and grate the potatoes. Peel and chop the onion. Mix together in a large basin or casserole dish. Cover with a plate or lid and cook on full power for 8 minutes.

2 Turn the corned beef out of the can and cut into cubes. Add to the potato mixture. Sprinkle in some salt and pepper. Use a wooden spoon to mix all the ingredients together really well.

3 Turn the mixture into a deep flan dish (not a very wide one) and press it down with a fork.

4 Cook on full power for 5 minutes, or until really hot.

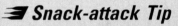 **Snack-attack Tip**

Heat up a can of baked beans or spaghetti hoops to go with the hash. Turn the beans or spaghetti into a basin and put a plate on top. Cook on full power for about 2-5 minutes, or until hot. Stir well before serving.

TASTY VEGETABLE DISHES

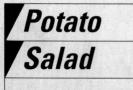

Potato Salad

SERVES 4

Ingredients

675 g/1½ lb potatoes
3 tablespoons water
150 ml/¼ pint mayonnaise
2 tablespoons milk
salt and pepper
2 tablespoons snipped
   chives

Cooking dish

casserole dish

Method

1 Peel the potatoes. Cut them in half, then cut them into cubes. Put the potatoes into a casserole dish with the water. Cover and cook on full power for 10 minutes.

2 Remove the dish from the oven using oven gloves. Carefully stir the potatoes, moving the pieces from the outside of the dish towards the middle. Cover the dish and cook for another 5 minutes on full power, or until tender. Drain off any water, then leave to cool.

3 Mix the mayonnaise with the milk. Add a little salt and pepper and the chives. Stir in the potatoes. Take care not to break the potatoes up. Turn the salad into a serving bowl and serve.

◢ Clever Cook's Tip

To prepare fresh chives, hold the bunch together and wash under cold water. Dry on absorbent kitchen paper. Hold one end firmly, then snip off the other end over a plate or small basin. Take care not to snip your fingers when you reach the end of the bunch.

Cheesy Corn-on-the-cob

SERVES 4

Ingredients

4 cobs of sweetcorn
75 g/3 oz cheese
50 g/2 oz butter
1 teaspoon made mustard

Cooking dishes

large casserole dish or large
   dish

Method

1 Take all the leaves and outer covering off the cobs of sweetcorn. Wash them and put in a large casserole dish or flan dish. The sweetcorn should be damp. Cover and cook on full power for 15 minutes, or until the sweetcorn is tender.

2 While the sweetcorn is cooking grate the cheese. Beat the butter with a wooden spoon until it is very soft. Beat in the cheese and mustard.

3 Use oven gloves to remove the sweetcorn from the microwave. Drain off any water. Place one cob of sweetcorn on each plate and put a spoonful of cheese mixture on top. Serve at once.

Prize Tomatoes

SERVES 4

Ingredients

8 small tomatoes
50 g/2 oz cheese
50 g/2 oz salted peanuts
50 g/2 oz fresh breadcrumbs
   (see page 31)
2 spring onions

Cooking dish

large plate

Method

1 Cut a thin slice off the tops of the tomatoes. Use a small teaspoon to scoop out the middle (seeds and pulp) of each tomato. Put this into a basin. Put a double-thick piece of absorbent kitchen paper on the work surface. Stand the tomatoes upside down on the paper to drain.

2 Grate the cheese. Roughly chop the peanuts. Mix the cheese, peanuts and breadcrumbs with the middle of the tomatoes.

3 Cut the roots and ends off the spring onions. Chop the rest and mix with the breadcrumbs and cheese. Using a teaspoon, divide this mixture between the tomato shells.

4 Put four of the stuffed tomatoes as far apart as possible on a small plate. Cook on full power for 2-2½ minutes, until the filling is just hot.

5 Cook the other four tomatoes in the same way. Serve at once.

Baked Potatoes

Timings are for large potatoes weighing about 350 g/12 oz each

Method

1 Scrub the potatoes and cut out any bad bits. You don't need a cooking dish, just a double-thick piece of absorbent kitchen paper. Put the paper on the turntable or on the floor of the oven.

2 Put the potatoes in the microwave, placing them as far apart as possible. Cook on full power, halfway through the cooking time open the oven and turn the potatoes over. Remember that they will be hot to hold, so use a clean tea-towel.

3 Cut a cross in the top of the cooked potatoes and put a knob of butter on top.

Cooking times

1 potato   7-8 minutes

2 potatoes   12 minutes

3 potatoes   15 minutes

4 potatoes   20-22 minutes

1 Cottage cheese (try the types with chives or other varieties).

3 Knob of butter and some sandwich spread.

5 Spoonful of mayonnaise and some prawns.

7 A slice of cooked ham, folded in half, and a few slices of tomato.

9 A spoonful of cream cheese and a few pieces of canned pineapple.

2 Cream cheese and chopped chives or spring onions.

4 Spoonful of chutney or your favourite relish and some grated cheese.

6 Slices of salami and some pickled onions, cut in half.

8 A spoonful of coleslaw.

10 A triangle of cheese spread with two slices of tomato and cucumber.

Baked Bean Specials

Ingredients

For each potato:

2 rindless rashers bacon
or 25 g/1 oz cheese
½ (227-g/8-oz) can baked beans
1 spring onion

Cooking dishes

large plate
small basin

Method

1 Before you cook the potato you will have to cook the bacon. Use a pair of kitchen scissors to cut the bacon rashers into thin strips. Put them on a large plate and cover with a piece of absorbent kitchen paper. Cook on full power for 4-5 minutes, or until very well cooked. Remove the paper as soon as you take the bacon from the microwave.

2 If you are using cheese, grate it while the potatoes are cooking.

3 Cook the potato. When it is ready, put the baked beans in a basin. Cover and cook on full power for 1½-2 minutes or until hot.

4 Split the potato almost through. Fill with the baked beans and top with bacon or cheese – you can always add both! Chop the spring onion and sprinkle on top.

Timing for 2, 3 or 4 servings:

4 rashers bacon
6-7 minutes

6 rashers bacon
8-10 minutes

8 rashers bacon
11-12 minutes

1 (227-g/8-oz) can beans
2-2½ minutes

1 (425-g/15-oz) can beans
4-5 minutes

Cottage Potatoes

Ingredients

For each baked potato:

50 g/2 oz cottage cheese
1 spring onion
a few salted peanuts

Method

1 While the potato is cooking put the cottage cheese in a basin. Cut the ends off the spring onion, wash the rest. Chop the spring onion and mix it with the cottage cheese.

2 Cut the cooked potato almost in half. Put the cottage cheese mixture in the potato and sprinkle with the peanuts. Serve at once.

Cheese 'n' Onion

Ingredients

For each potato:

50 g/2 oz cheese
½ small onion
a little chopped parsley

Method

1 While the potato is cooking grate the cheese. Cut the onion into very thin slices, then separate these into strips.

2 Cut the cooked potato almost in half. Fill the middle with the grated cheese. Top with the onion and parsley.

Frankfurt Corn Filling

Ingredients

For each potato:

50 g/2 oz frozen sweetcorn
1 frankfurter
1 spring onion
1 tomato
salt and pepper
knob of butter

Cooking dish

large basin

Method

1 First cook the potato. While it is cooking, put the sweetcorn in a basin to cook in the microwave. Slice the frankfurter. Trim the ends off the spring onion and chop it up. Cut the tomato in half, then cut each half into small pieces.

2 Cook the sweetcorn on full power for the following times:

50 g/2 oz   1½ minutes
100 g/4 oz   2-2½ minutes
175 g/6 oz   3-4 minutes
225 g/8 oz   4-5 minutes

Drain the cooked sweetcorn through a sieve or colander. Put it back in the basin.

3 Add the frankfurter to the sweetcorn and heat for 1-3 minutes. When the frankfurter slices are hot stir in the tomato and spring onion. Add a little salt and pepper.

4 Cut the cooked potatoes almost in half. Fill with the sweetcorn mixture and top with a knob of butter. Serve at once.

Creamy Vegy Filling

Ingredients

For each potato:

50 g/2 oz frozen mixed vegetables
50 g/2 oz cream cheese
mayonnaise or salad cream
a few packet croûtons

Cooking dish

small basin

Method

1 First cook the potato. Put the frozen mixed vegetables in a basin and cover. Cook on full power for the following times:

50 g/2 oz   1-2 minutes
100 g/4 oz   2-3 minutes
175 g/6 oz   3-4 minutes
225 g/8 oz   4-5 minutes

2 While the vegetables are cooking, mix the cream cheese with a little mayonnaise or salad cream to soften the cheese slightly.

3 Drain the cooked vegetables in a sieve or colander. Split the potatoes almost in half. Fill with vegetables and top with the cream cheese. Sprinkle with croûtons if you like.

Cheese Sauce

MAKES 300 ml/½ pint

Ingredients

2 tablespoons flour
300 ml/½ pint milk
15 g/½ oz butter or
    margarine
salt and pepper
75 g/3 oz cheese

Cooking dish

large basin (to hold
    1.12 litres/2 pints)

Method

1 Put the flour in a large basin. Make sure that it is big enough for the sauce to boil up. Stirring all the time, slowly pour in a little of the milk to make a smooth paste. Pour in all the milk when you are sure there are no lumps in the paste.

2 Stir in the butter or margarine and a little salt and pepper. Cook on full power for 3 minutes. Whisk well and cook on full power for another 2 minutes, or until the sauce boils.

3 Grate the cheese. Stir it into the sauce and cook on full power for 1 minute. Stir well and use the sauce in a recipe or to serve with a main dish.

Cauliflower Cheese

SERVES 4

Ingredients

1 medium cauliflower
cheese sauce (see recipe, left)
2 tablespoons browned breadcrumbs (see page 31)

Cooking dishes

large casserole dish
large basin

Method

1 Cut the outer green stalks off the cauliflower. Wash it thoroughly under cold running water. Put the wet cauliflower in a large casserole dish and cover the dish. Cook on full power for 14-16 minutes, or until the cauliflower is tender but not too soft. Use oven gloves to lift the dish from the microwave.

2 Make the cheese sauce following the recipe carefully. Using a fish slice and large spoon, lift the cauliflower into a colander or sieve over a sink and drain. Put the cauliflower back in the empty dish and pour the sauce over. Sprinkle the breadcrumbs over the top. Cook on full power for 2-3 minutes until the cauliflower is hot. Serve at once.

Hi-speed Tip

Sometimes you can drain the cauliflower by holding the lid of the casserole firmly, leaving a small gap. Tilt the casserole over the sink to drain off the liquid.

Savoury Mushrooms

SERVES 4

Ingredients

4 very large open
  mushrooms
100 g/4 oz frozen peas
50 g/2 oz fresh breadcrumbs
2 large spring onions
salt and pepper
2 tablespoons milk
4 rindless rashers bacon

Cooking dishes

large basin
flan dish or large shallow
  dish

Method

1 Wipe the mushrooms and
cut off their stalks. Chop the
stalks and put in a large
basin. Stir in the frozen peas
and breadcrumbs.

2 Cut the roots off the spring
onions and trim the tops,
then chop the rest. Add to
the peas and breadcrumbs.
Season with salt and pepper.
Stir in the milk.

3 Put the mushrooms, open
side up, in a flan dish or any
wide, shallow dish. Use a
teaspoon to put the stuffing
on the mushrooms, pressing
it down firmly.

4 Roll up each rasher of
bacon quite tightly. Place a
bacon roll on top of each
mushroom, pressing each
one firmly in place.

Saucy Leeks

SERVES 4

Ingredients

450 g/1 lb leeks
cheese sauce (see recipe on
  page 29)
salt and pepper
4 rindless rashers bacon
4 tablespoons browned
  breadcrumbs
2 tomatoes

Cooking dishes

casserole dish
large basin
small basin

Method

1 Trim the ends off the
leeks. Make a cut halfway
into each leek down the
long side. Wash under
running water.

2 Put the wet leeks in a
casserole dish. Cover and
cook on full power for 10-12
minutes.

3 Make the cheese sauce
following the recipe. Pour
the sauce over the leeks and
stir in a little salt and pepper.

4 Cut the bacon rashers
across into small strips.
Place in a small basin and
cook on full power for 5
minutes.

5 Stir the breadcrumbs into
the bacon. Cut the tomatoes
in half, then cut them into
small pieces. Stir the
tomatoes into the bacon
mixture.

6 Spoon the mixture over the
top of the leeks. Cook on full
power for 2 minutes. Serve
with crusty bread.

5 Cook on full power for about 10 minutes so that the bacon rolls are cooked through. Leave to stand for 2 minutes before serving. If any of the bacon rolls slip off the top of the mushrooms, use a spoon and fork to lift them back on top before you serve the mushrooms.

◢ Clever Cook's Tip

To make breadcrumbs, rub a chunk of bread on the coarse side of a grater. For brown breadcrumbs, sprinkle them on a piece of cooking foil and put them under a hot grill. Watch in case they burn. Leave to cool, then mix them with your fingers.

Vegetable Lasagne

SERVES 4

Ingredients

cheese sauce (see page 29)
1 leek
15 g/½ oz butter
175 g/6 oz cauliflower florets
225 g/8 oz courgettes
50 g/2 oz mushrooms
1 (400-g/14-oz) can chopped
  tomatoes
2 teaspoons marjoram
salt and pepper
about 8 pieces no-cook
  lasagne
2 tablespoons browned
  breadcrumbs

Cooking dishes

2 large basins
large casserole dish or
  lasagne dish

Method

1 Make the cheese sauce following the recipe.

2 Cut the ends off the leek, then cut it into thin slices. Put these in a colander or sieve and wash well under cold running water. Put the leeks in a large basin. Add the butter.

3 Wash the cauliflower and cut into pieces. Add to the leek and cook on full power for 4 minutes.

4 Wash the courgettes. Trim off the ends, then cut them in half lengthways. Cut the halves into thin slices.

5 Wipe the mushrooms with a damp cloth, then slice them. Add the courgettes and mushrooms to the leek and cauliflower. Stir in the chopped tomatoes. Mix in the marjoram and seasoning.

6 Put a layer of the lasagne in a deep casserole dish or in a lasagne dish. Cover with half the vegetables. Add a second layer of lasagne and the rest of the vegetables.

7 Lay the remaining pieces of lasagne on top of the vegetables. Make sure that the dish is not too full. Pour the sauce over the top and spread it evenly.

8 Cook the lasagne on medium power for 20-25 minutes. Leave to stand for 5 minutes. The pasta should be soft. Sprinkle with browned breadcrumbs.

Stuffed Courgettes

SERVES 4

Ingredients

1 onion
15 g/½ oz butter
4 medium courgettes
50 g/2 oz nuts (walnuts, cashew nuts, peanuts or mixed nuts)
50 g/2 oz cheese
75 g/3 oz fresh breadcrumbs (see page 31)
salt and pepper

Cooking dishes

large basin
large flan dish

Method

1 Peel and chop the onion. Put it in a large basin with butter and cook on full power for 3 minutes.

2 Wash and dry the courgettes. Carefully cut them in half lengthways. Use a teaspoon to scoop out the middle. Cut this up and add it to the onion. Cook on full power for another 4 minutes.

3 Chop the nuts. Grate the cheese. Mix the breadcrumbs, nuts and cheese into the onion and courgette mixture. Add a little salt and pepper – take care – if you used salted nuts you may not need salt.

4 Put four of the courgette shells in a large flan dish or a shallow dish. Use a teaspoon to put the stuffing in the courgettes. Press it down well – remember to use only half the mixture.

5 Cook the four shells on full power for 4 minutes, or until the outside is cooked and the filling is hot.

6 While the first four are cooking, press the rest of the stuffing into the remaining courgette halves.

7 Lift the cooked courgettes on to plates. Put the uncooked courgettes into the dish. Cook them in the same way as the first four.

Cabbage Rolls

SERVES 4

Ingredients

4 large cabbage leaves
4 tablespoons water
175 g/6 oz carrots
175 g/6 oz potatoes
1 onion
25 g/oz butter
100 g/4 oz cheese
1 egg
salt and pepper
6 tablespoons fresh breadcrumbs (see page 31)
½ teaspoon dried mixed herbs
2 tomatoes

Cooking dishes

flan dish
casserole dish

Method

1 Wash the cabbage leaves and put them in a flan dish. Sprinkle the water over the cabbage. Cover the dish with microwave cling film or a plate turned upside down, leaving a small gap. Cook on full power for 7 minutes. Use oven gloves to lift the dish from the microwave. Set aside.

2 Peel and grate the carrots, potatoes and onion. Mix all the grated vegetables in a casserole dish. Add the butter and cover the dish. Cook on full power for 10-12 minutes, or until softened.

3 While the vegetables are cooking grate the cheese. Add it to the hot vegetables and stir well. Stir in the egg and add salt and pepper.

4 Drain the cabbage leaves in a colander or sieve. Lay them flat on a clean surface. Divide the carrot mixture between the leaves, piling it up in the middle of each one. Roll up the leaves neatly, then arrange them in the casserole dish.

5 Mix the breadcrumbs and the herbs. Cut the tomatoes in half, then cut each half into small pieces. Add to the breadcrumbs. Spoon this over the cabbage rolls.

6 Cover the dish and cook on full power 6-7 minutes, or until hot.

Pepper Boats

S E R V E S 4

Ingredients

1 onion
2 large green peppers
175 g/6 oz carrots
1 eating apple
225 g/8 oz sausagemeat
100 g/4 oz frozen peas
salt and pepper
1 teaspoon dried sage

Cooking dishes

large basin
flan dish or large casserole
dish

Method

1 Peel and chop the onion. Put it in a large basin and cover with a plate. Cook on full power for 3 minutes.

2 While the onion is cooking, cut the peppers in half through the stalk. Use a small knife to cut out the core. Rinse out the seeds and dry the pepper shells. Arrange the peppers in a flan dish or in a large casserole dish cut side up.

3 Grate the carrots. Peel the apple, cut it into quarters and cut out the cores. Chop the apple into small pieces.

4 Add the sausagemeat, carrots, apple and peas to the onion. Use a wooden spoon to mix all the ingredients together well. Add a little salt and pepper and the sage, then stir to mix the ingredients.

5 Divide the mixture into four. Put a portion of the mixture into each of the pepper boats. Press it in with a teaspoon.

6 Cover the dish with microwave cling film or a lid and cook on full power for 15 minutes. Leave to stand for 3 minutes before serving.

SPEEDY SUPPERS

Scrambled Eggs

Ingredients

For 1 small portion:

1 egg
2 tablespoons milk
salt and pepper
knob of butter

For 1 large portion, or 2 small portions:

2 eggs
4 tablespoons milk
salt and pepper
knob of butter

For 2-3 portions:

3 eggs
6 tablespoons milk
salt and pepper
knob of butter

For 2 large portions, or 4 small portions:

4 eggs
8 tablespoons milk
salt and pepper
knob of butter

Cooking dish

large basin

Method

1 If you want to make toast with the scrambled eggs, cut the bread first. Put it under the grill or in the toaster ready to cook as you are making the eggs.

2 Beat the egg and milk with salt and pepper in a large basin. Add a knob of butter and cook on full power for the times given below.

3 Watch the egg as it cooks. When the edges start to set and bubble up, take the basin from the microwave and whisk the eggs well. Put them back and cook again until setting and bubbling. When ready, the egg should still be slightly runny.

4 Leave to stand for 1 minute before serving. You should whisk the egg about three or four times during cooking, depending on how many you are cooking.

Cooking times

1 egg	45-60 seconds
2 eggs	2-2¼ minutes
3 eggs	2½-3 minutes
4 eggs	4-4½ minutes

Hi-speed Tip

Cook the toast at step 3. Butter it and put it on the plate when the eggs are standing after cooking.

Super Scramblers

Try adding some of these ingredients to the scrambled eggs before serving them. Prepare the ingredients *before* you cook the eggs so that they are ready to stir in as soon as the eggs are cooked.

For each egg:

- 2 tablespoons grated cheese
- 1 chopped tomato
- 2 tablespoons chopped cooked ham
- 1 chopped spring onion
- 2 tablespoons flaked tuna fish
- 1 tablespoon chopped parsley

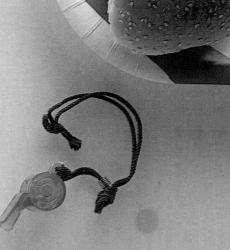

Serving Ideas

You don't have to put the eggs on toast – try some of these ideas for a change. Remember to get them ready before you cook the eggs.

On buttered Dutch crispbread.

On a split buttered burger bun.

In tomato shells – cut the tops off large tomatoes and scoop out the middle using a teaspoon. Fill with scrambled egg.

In baked potatoes – see page 26 for the recipes.

In sandwiches – scrambled eggs make terrific sandwiches. You can use the eggs hot or cold.

On split French bread – fresh or toasted.

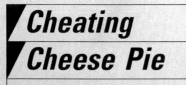

Cheating Cheese Pie

SERVES 4

Ingredients

1 (90-g/3½-oz) packet instant
   mashed potato
450 ml/¾ pint cold water
1 small onion
1 small egg
100 g/4 oz cheese
salt and pepper
4 tablespoons browned
   breadcrumbs (see page 31)
50 g/cooked ham

Cooking dishes

large basin
large souffle dish or deep
   round dish

Method

1 Put the instant mashed potato into a large basin. Pour in the cold water. Peel and grate the onion, then stir it into the potato. Cook on full power for 6-8 minutes, or until the mixture is like proper mashed potato.

2 Beat the egg in a small basin. Use oven gloves to remove the potato from the microwave. Stir in the beaten egg.

3 Grate the cheese. Save some to sprinkle over the top of the pie and stir the rest into the potato. Stir in a little salt and pepper.

4 Spoon the mixture into a soufflé dish and smooth the top. Mix the breadcrumbs with the cheese. Chop the cooked ham and stir it into the breadcrumb mixture. Sprinkle this over the top of the potato.

5 Cook on full power for 5 minutes, or until hot. Leave to stand for a few minutes before serving.

Hot Ham Rolls

SERVES 4

Ingredients

2 small tomatoes
100 g/4 oz cream cheese
4 tablespoons sage and
   onion stuffing mix
4 slices cooked ham
100 g/4 oz frozen peas
100 g/4 oz frozen sweetcorn

Cooking dish

casserole dish

Method

1 Cut the tomatoes in half. Place them cut side down on a chopping board and cut them into small pieces.

2 Beat the tomatoes and cream cheese together in a basin. Stir in the sage and onion stuffing mix. Divide the mixture into four.

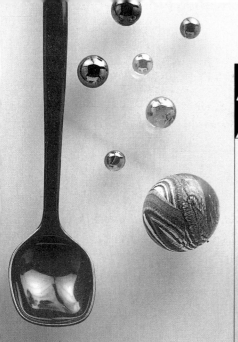

3 Spread a portion of the mixture over each of the slices of ham and roll up.

4 Mix the frozen peas and sweetcorn in a casserole dish. Lay the ham rolls on top and cover the dish. Cook on full power for 4-5 minutes. The vegetables and ham rolls should be hot.

➤ Hi-speed Tip

During cooking, the ham rolls may make loud popping noises – don't worry, it is caused by the heat building up inside the rolls. If the dish is covered, there will be no splattering in the oven.

Fisherman's Flan

SERVES 4

Ingredients

100 g/4 oz butter
225 g/8 oz crackers or cheese biscuits

Filling

1 onion
15 g/½ oz butter
50 g/2 oz mushrooms
2 tablespoons flour
150 ml/¼ pint milk
salt and pepper
50 g/2 oz cheese
1 (198-g/7-oz) can tuna
2 tomatoes

Cooking dishes

large basin
20-cm/8-in flan dish

Method

1 Put the butter in a large basin and cook on full power for 2 minutes, until melted.

2 Put the crackers or cheese biscuits in a polythene bag and crush them carefully with a rolling pin. Stir them into the melted butter.

3 Press the biscuits on the base and up round the sides of the flan dish.

4 Make the filling. Peel and chop the onion. Place it in the basin with the butter and cook on full power for 3 minutes.

5 Wipe the mushrooms with a damp cloth then slice them. Stir the flour into the onion, then slowly stir in the milk. Stir well to get rid of lumps. Add seasoning and the mushrooms.

6 Grate the cheese and stir it into the sauce. Cook on full power for 2 minutes. Stir well to make sure the sauce is smooth.

7 Drain the tuna, then add it to the sauce and break it into pieces using a fork. Cook for 2-3 minutes, or until the sauce is thick and hot.

8 Spoon the sauce into the flan and cook for 2 minutes. Meanwhile, slice the tomatoes. Arrange the tomatoes round the edge of the flan and serve at once.

Savoury Fish Cakes

S E R V E S 4

Ingredients

1 (124-g/4⅜-oz) can sardines
   in tomato sauce
50 g/2 oz cheese
100 g/4 oz fresh
   breadcrumbs (see page 31)
salt and pepper
1 tablespoon lemon juice
2 tablespoons milk
50 g/2 oz browned
   breadcrumbs (see page 31)
large sprig of watercress to
   garnish

Cooking dish

large plate

Method

1 Open the can of sardines, turn them into a basin and mash them with a fork.

2 Grate the cheese. Mix it into the sardines. Add the breadcrumbs and a little salt and pepper. Mix in the lemon juice and milk to soften the mixture.

3 Divide the mixture into eight equal portions. Sprinkle the browned bread-crumbs on a plate.

4 Wet your hands, then shape a portion of the mixture into a small, thin cake about 7 cm/2 in in diameter. Press the cake in the browned breadcrumbs to cover it all over. Make the other fish cakes in the same way.

5 Put four fish cakes on a large plate, putting them as far apart as possible round the edge of the plate. Cover with a piece of absorbent kitchen paper and cook on full power for 3 minutes, or until hot. Use a fish slice to lift the fish cakes on to a serving plate and cook the others in the same way.

6 Garnish with a large sprig of watercress and serve.

Captain's Kebabs

S E R V E S 4

Ingredients

4 frozen cod steaks
2 medium courgettes
2 spring onions
2 teaspoons lemon juice
25 g/1 oz butter
salt and pepper

Cooking dishes

flan dish
4 wooden skewers

Method

1 Leave the cod steaks until they are just beginning to soften but do not let them thaw completely.

2 Wash the courgettes. Cut off the ends, then cut them into fairly thick slices. Trim the spring onions and use a pair of scissors to cut them into small pieces.

3 Cut each cod steak into six cubes. Thread the cubes of fish and the slices of courgette alternately on to four wooden skewers. Lay them in a flan dish. Sprinkle the lemon juice over and dot with the butter.

4 Cover with microwave cling film or an upturned plate, leaving a small gap for the steam to escape. Cook on full power for 3 minutes. Use oven gloves to lift the dish from the microwave.

5 Turn the kebabs over. Cover with fresh microwave cling film or the plate, leaving a gap for the steam to escape. Cook on full power for another 2-3 minutes, or until the fish is cooked.

6 Sprinkle the spring onions and a little salt and pepper over the kebabs before serving.

Bubble and Squeak with Bacon

SERVES 4

Ingredients

225 g/8 oz potatoes
1 onion
225 g/8 oz cabbage
2 tablespoons water
225 g/8 oz rindless bacon
25 g/ oz butter

Cooking dish

large casserole dish

Method

1 Peel the potatoes and cut them into small cubes. Peel and chop the onion. Shred the cabbage.

2 Put the potatoes, onion and cabbage in a large casserole dish. Add the water and cover the dish. Cook on full power for 15 minutes.

3 Cut across the bacon rashers to give small strips. Use oven gloves to lift the casserole from the oven. Add the bacon to the potato mixture and stir well. Cover the dish and cook for 5 minutes.

4 Again using oven gloves, remove the casserole from the microwave. Stir the mixture well, then flatten it, pressing down with the back of a spoon. Dot with butter. Cook, uncovered, on full power for 5 minutes. Leave for 2 minutes before serving.

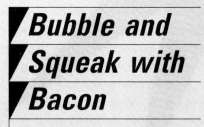

Sweet 'n' Sour Ham Baps

SERVES 4

Ingredients

1 (227-g/8-oz) can pineapple rings in syrup
2 tablespoons tomato ketchup
a little vinegar
4 baps or hamburger buns
4 small, thick slices cooked ham
2 thin slices onion

Cooking dish

large plate

Method

1 Open the can of pineapple and drain the syrup into a cup. Mix 1 tablespoon of this syrup with the ketchup and a little vinegar.

2 Split the baps in half. Put the bottom halves on a large plate. Put a slice of ham on each half. Top the ham with with a pineapple ring.

3 Separate the onion slices into rings and divide them between the baps. Spoon a little of the sauce over the filling, then press the lids on the baps. Cook on full power for 2 minutes, or until hot. Serve at once.

39

Peanut Rice

Ingredients

1 onion
175 g/6 oz carrots
100 g/4 oz rice
salt and pepper
300 ml/½ pint water
1 (198-g/7-oz) can sweetcorn
75 g/3 oz salted peanuts

Cooking dish

large basin or casserole dish

Method

1 Peel and chop the onion. Cut the ends off the carrots and scrub them under running water. Cut the carrots into small cubes.

2 Put the onion, carrots and rice in a large basin or casserole dish. Stir in salt and pepper and pour in the water. Cover and cook on full power for 10 minutes.

3 Drain the can of sweetcorn. Add the sweetcorn and nuts to the rice, using a fork to mix them in very lightly. Cover again and cook on full power for a further 3-4 minutes. Leave for 2 minutes before serving.

Risotto

S E R V E S   4

Ingredients

1 large onion
225 g/8 oz easy-cook long-
     grain rice
1 chicken stock cube
100 g/4 oz frozen sweetcorn
600 ml/1 pint water
100 g/4 oz cooked ham
100 g/4 oz frozen cut beans
salt and pepper

Cooking dish

large casserole dish

Method

1 Peel and chop the onion. Put it in a casserole dish with the rice. Crumble the stock cube into the dish and add the sweetcorn. Pour in the water. Stir well and cover the dish. Cook on full power for 15 minutes.

2 While the rice is cooking, cut the ham into small pieces. Use oven gloves to remove the dish from the microwave.

3 Add the ham, beans and a little salt and pepper to the dish. Use a fork to lightly mix these ingredients into the rice. Cover the dish and cook on full power for another 10-12 minutes, or until most of the water has been absorbed. The risotto should be moist. Leave to stand for 2 minutes before serving.

Hi-speed Tip

You can add all sorts of ingredients to risotto. Cut up cooked left-over meat or chicken and add it with the beans. Add chopped tomatoes and shredded cabbage if you like. Roughly chopped nuts and sultanas or raisins also taste good. Sliced mushrooms can be added with the beans. Serve some grated cheese in a small bowl to sprinkle over the risotto just before it is eaten.

Simple Pizza

SERVES 4

Ingredients

1 onion
1 tablespoon oil
1 tablespoon tomato purée
1 teaspoon marjoram
salt and pepper
75 g/3 oz cheese
100 g/4 oz self-raising flour
25 g/1 oz butter or margarine
1 egg
1 tablespoon milk
1 tablespoon chopped
   parsley to garnish

Cooking dishes

small basin
large flan dish or flat plate

Method

1 Peel and chop the onion. Put it in a basin with the oil. Cover and cook on full power for 3 minutes. Stir in the tomato purée and the marjoram. Add a little salt and pepper. Set aside. Grate the cheese.

2 Put the flour in a bowl. Add the butter or margarine and cut it into two or three pieces. Using just the tips of your fingers, rub the fat into the flour. Lift the mixture into the air as you rub. The rubbed in ingredients should look like fine breadcrumbs.

3 Lightly beat the egg. Mix the egg and milk into the dry ingredients to make a soft dough.

4 Put a little flour on the work surface. Turn the dough on to it and knead it into a ball. Do this very lightly and very quickly.

5 Sprinkle a little flour on a rolling pin and roll out the dough to give a circle measuring about 20 cm/8 in across.

6 Lightly grease a large flan dish. Lift the circle of dough on to it. Pinch up the edges of the dough to help the filling to stay on top.

7 Spread the tomato mixture all over the dough. Sprinkle the cheese on top, leaving just the edge uncovered. Cook on full power for 3½-4 minutes. The edge of the dough should be risen and the dough cooked through. The cheese should have melted. Sprinkle with parsley and serve.

Tempting Toppings

Try some of the following toppings. Sprinkle them over the pizza, on top of the tomato mixture; sprinkle the cheese on top and cook as above.

Mushrooms wipe and slice 50 g/2 oz mushrooms.

Cooked ham roughly chop 50 g/2 oz cooked ham.

Tuna drain and flake a 75-g/3-oz can tuna fish.

Salami cut 25 g/1 oz sliced salami into thin strips.

Sweetcorn add 50 g/2 oz frozen sweetcorn (this is good with chopped ham too!)

Anchovies drain 1 (50-g/2-oz) can anchovies and put them on top of the cheese.

Olives add about 8 stoned olives (stuffed green ones are good) on top of the cheese.

41

SNAPPY SNACKS

Hungry Horse Sandwich

MAKES 1

Ingredients

a little butter
2 slices bread
1 rindless rasher bacon
1 tomato

Cooking dish

large plate

Method

1 Lightly butter the bread. Put the bacon on a large plate and lay a piece of absorbent kitchen paper over it. Cook on full power for 1-1½ minutes, or until the bacon is cooked.

2 While the bacon is cooking slice the tomato. Cut the cooked bacon rasher in half and lay it on one slice of bread. Top with the tomato and the second slice of bread. Yum!

Snack-attack Tip

Add cheese, cucumber, tomato ketchup, or relish.

Crumpet Burgers

Ingredients

For each burger:

1 small frozen beefburger
1 tablespoon chutney or relish
1 crumpet
25 g/1 oz cheese
1 tablespoon mayonnaise
sprig of parsley to garnish

Cooking dish

large plate

Method

1 The cooking times are for burgers which weigh about 50 g/2 oz each. Spread the relish or chutney on the crumpet and put the beefburger on top.

2 Place the crumpet burger on a plate and cook for the following times:

1 burger   3-4 minutes
2 burgers   5 minutes
3 burgers   6-7 minutes
4 burgers   8 minutes

3 While the burgers are cooking, grate the cheese and mix it with the mayonnaise. Top the burger with this mixture. Add a sprig of parsley and eat at once!

Cracker Snacks

MAKES 12

Ingredients

1 small eating apple
50 g/2 oz cheese
2 tablespoons peanut butter
2 teaspoons snipped chives
salt and pepper
12 crackers

Cooking dish

large plate

Method

1 Peel the apple thinly. Holding both ends of the apple, grate the flesh off the core.

2 Grate the cheese. Mix the apple and cheese with the peanut butter and chives. When the ingredients begin to bind together, beat well. Add a little salt and pepper.

3 Spread the mixture over the crackers. Put four on a large plate and cook each batch for 30 seconds on full power. Watch them as they cook – they are ready as soon as the cheese melts.

◢ Snack-attack Tip

If you like spicy food add ¼ teaspoon curry powder to the mixture.

Hot Dogs

SERVES 4

Ingredients

1 onion
25 g/1 oz butter or margarine
4 frankfurters
4 long rolls
ketchup or mustard to serve

Cooking dish

large basin

Method

1 Peel and chop the onion. Put it in a large basin with the butter or margarine. Cook on full power for 3-5 minutes.

2 Put the frankfurters in the basin on top of the onions and cook on full power for 2-3 minutes, until hot.

3 Split the rolls and put a frankfurter in each. Use a spoon to divide the onion between the hot dogs. Spread a little tomato ketchup or mustard over the hot dogs if you like.

Topping Pitta

S E R V E S 4

Ingredients

4 rindless bacon rashers
4 tablespoons peanut butter
4 pieces pitta bread
2 tomatoes

Cooking dish

large plate

Method

1 Cut the bacon rashers in half. Spread the peanut butter on top of the pitta bread and cover with bacon. Place two on a large plate and cook on full power for 2-3 minutes, or until the bacon is cooked.

2 While the pitta bread is cooking slice the tomatoes. Cook the two remaining pieces of pitta bread in the same way as the first pair. Top with slices of tomato and serve. You'll need knives and forks to eat this snack otherwise it can be very messy!

Scrumptious Crumpets

S E R V E S 4

Ingredients

100 g/4 oz cheese
1 tablespoon tomato ketchup
1 teaspoon made mustard
dash of Worcestershire
    sauce
8 crumpets
cucumber slices to garnish

Cooking dish

large plate

Method

1 Grate the cheese and put it in a bowl. Add the ketchup, mustard and Worcestershire sauce. Use a wooden spoon to mix all the ingredients together really well.

2 Spread the cheese mixture over the crumpets. Put four on a large plate and cook on full power for about 3 minutes, or until the cheese mixture has melted and the crumpets are hot. Cook the other four in the same way.

3 Top each crumpet with cucumber slices and serve.

Breakfast Waffles

SERVES 4

Ingredients

2 rindless rashers bacon
50 g/2 oz cheese
4 frozen potato waffles
1 (225-g/8-oz) can baked
  beans

Cooking dish

large flan dish

Method

1 Using a pair of kitchen scissors, cut across the bacon rashers to make thin strips. Grate the cheese.

2 Put the potato waffles on a flat dish – a large flan dish is best. Cook on full power for 2 minutes.

3 Divide the baked beans between the waffles. Place the strips of bacon on top, then sprinkle the grated cheese over the bacon. Cook on full power for 4-5 minutes, or until they are bubbling hot.

◀ Snack-attack Tip

These breakfast waffles taste fantastic at any time of the day! You can use chopped cooked ham or corned beef instead of bacon, or try adding some sliced frankfurters instead. In place of the baked beans you could use spaghetti hoops or canned pasta shapes in sauce.

Speedy Toasties

SERVES 4

Ingredients

4 Dutch crispbreads
1 eating apple
4 thick slices cheese
4 parsley sprigs to garnish

Cooking dish

large plate or shallow dish

Method

1 Put the Dutch crispbreads as far apart as possible on a large plate or shallow dish.

2 Cut the ends off the apple, then cut it into four thick slices. Use the point of a knife to cut out the core.

3 Put a slice of apple and a slice of cheese on each crispbread. Cook on full power for 1-1½ minutes, or until the cheese has melted. Top with parsley sprigs and serve.

Bangers 'n' Beans

S E R V E S 4

Ingredients

8 skinless sausages
1 onion
25 g/1 oz butter
1 (447-g/15-oz) can baked
  beans
hot toast to serve

Cooking dish

large basin

Method

1 Cut each sausage into three. Peel and chop the onion. Place the onion and the butter in a large basin. Cook on full power for 3 minutes.

2 Stir the sausages into the onion. Cook on full power for 4 minutes. Use oven gloves to lift the basin from the microwave. Stir the sausages, then cook on full power for another 4 minutes.

3 Pour the baked beans into the basin and stir well. Cover the basin with a plate and cook on full power for 3-4 minutes to heat the beans.

4 Make the toast while the beans are cooking – do this in a toaster or under the grill as you would normally. Butter the toast and put it on the plates.

5 Spoon the bangers and beans over the toast and serve at once.

Hot Sardine Bread

S E R V E S 4

Ingredients

1 (124-g/4⅜-oz) can sardines
  in tomato sauce
50 g/2 oz cream cheese
salt and pepper
pinch of dried mixed herbs
½ French loaf

Cooking dish

large plate

Method

1 Put the sardines and their sauce in a basin and mash them with a fork. Add the cream cheese and use the fork to mix it with the sardines. Stir in salt and pepper and the dried herbs.

2 Cut almost through the French bread to slice it into pieces, leaving each slice attached at the base. Spread the sardine mixture on the slices, pressing the pieces back together.

3 Put the bread on a large plate and cook on full power for 2-2½ minutes, or until hot. Cut between the slices to separate them and serve.

➤ Hi-speed Tip

You can make garlic bread in the same way as the sardine bread. Use butter instead of cream cheese and mix in plenty of chopped fresh herbs, or a crushed clove of garlic.

Stir-fry Specials

S E R V E S   4

Ingredients

1 courgette
1 small onion
1 carrot
3 frankfurters
1 tablespoon oil
4 pieces pitta bread
a little soy sauce

Cooking dishes

large basin or casserole dish
large plate

Method

1 Trim the ends off the courgette. Cut it in half lengthways, then cut each half into three. Slice each piece thinly to make long strips.

2 Peel the onion and cut it in half, then cut each half into thin slices. Trim the carrot, cut it in half lengthways. Cut each half across into two, then slice the pieces into thin strips. Slice the frankfurters.

3 Put all the vegetables and frankfurters in a large basin or casserole dish. Add the oil and mix well. Cover with a plate or lid and cook on full power for 3-4 minutes, or until lightly cooked and hot.

4 Put the pitta bread on a large plate and lay a piece of absorbent kitchen paper on top. Cook on full power for 1 minute.

5 Mix the vegetables well and sprinkle with a little soy sauce. Split the pitta bread down one side, then use a spoon to put the stir-fry mixture into the bread. Eat at once!

FAVOURITE PUDDINGS

Banana Splits

MAKES 4

Ingredients

100 g/4 oz plain chocolate
2 tablespoons milk
4 tablespoons golden syrup
4 small bananas
8 scoops ice cream
8 glacé cherries
4 wafer biscuits

Cooking dish

basin or large measuring jug

Method

1 Break the chocolate into squares and place them in a basin or large measuring jug. Add the milk and the golden syrup. Cook on full power for 1 minute, then stir lightly. Cook for another ½-1 minute, until the chocolate has melted and the sauce is hot. Stir well until smooth.

2 Peel the bananas and cut them in half lengthways. Place the halves slightly apart on four long dishes. Put 2 scoops of ice cream between the pieces of banana on each dish.

3 Pour some chocolate sauce over the ice cream. Top with glacé cherries and add a wafer biscuit to each banana split. Serve at once.

Dessert Idea

This chocolate sauce tastes great with all sorts of ice cream. It is also good with waffles or with canned fruit for a quick pud.

Apple Special

SERVES 4

Ingredients

450 g/1 lb cooking apples
75 g/3 oz sugar
2 tablespoons water
50 g/2 oz raisins
50 g/2 oz walnuts

Cooking dish

large casserole dish

Method

1 Cut the apples into quarters. Cut off the peel as thinly as you can. Cut out the core and slice the apples into a large casserole dish.

2 Add the sugar, water and raisins. Cover the dish and cook on full power for 5 minutes, or until the apples are soft.

3 Roughly chop the walnuts. Stir the apple, then divide it between four dishes. Sprinkle the nuts on and serve with cream or ice cream.

Wapples

SERVES 4

Ingredients

2 medium cooking apples
a little lemon juice
4 tablespoons brown sugar
1 teaspoon ground
   cinnamon
8 frozen waffles
25 g/1 oz butter
150 ml/¼ pint thick (Greek)
   natural yogurt

Cooking dish

flan dish

Method

1 Cut the ends off the apples, then cut each one into four thick slices. Use the point of a knife to cut the core out of the middle of each slice. Sprinkle with a little lemon juice to stop the apple from going brown.

2 Mix the sugar with the cinnamon. Put four waffles on a flan dish. Put a slice of apple on each, then sprinkle a little of the sugar mixture on top. Dot with butter and cook on full power for 1½-2 minutes, or until the butter and sugar are melted and the apple soft. Top each wapple with a spoonful of creamy yogurt and serve. Cook the other four wapples while you eat the first batch.

Banana and Peach Crumble

SERVES 4

Ingredients

1 (227-g/8-oz) can peach
   slices
2 large bananas
50 g/2 oz plain flour
25 g/1 oz margarine or butter
1 tablespoon sugar
75 g/3 oz chocolate digestive
   biscuits
50 g/2 oz toasted chopped
   hazelnuts

Cooking dish

15-cm/6-in soufflé dish or
   small casserole dish

Method

1 Pour the peaches and their syrup into a 15-cm/6-in soufflé dish or small casserole dish. Peel and slice the bananas, then mix them with the peaches.

2 Put the flour into a bowl. Add the margarine or butter and cut it into small pieces. Using just the tips of your fingers, rub the fat into the flour until the mixture resembles fine breadcrumbs. Lift the mixture into the air as you rub it between your fingers. Add the sugar to the mixture.

3 Put the biscuits in a polythene bag and use a rolling pin to crush them – take care not to burst the bag! Mix the biscuits and nuts into the crumble.

4 Spoon the crumble over the fruit to cover it completely. Cook on full power for 5-7 minutes, or until the topping is cooked.

5 Serve hot, with cream, ice cream or custard (see page 52).

Dotty Puddings

SERVES 4

Ingredients

75 g/3 oz soft margarine
75 g/3 oz caster sugar
75 g/3 oz self-raising flour
1 egg
3 tablespoons milk
50 g/2 oz chocolate drops for
   cooking

Cooking dishes

4 small heatproof basins
   (holding about 300 ml/
   ½ pint each)

Method

1 Put the margarine, sugar, flour and egg in a mixing bowl and beat well using a wooden spoon until very creamy and pale in colour. Scrape the mixture down into the middle of the bowl from time to time. Beat in the milk and stir in the chocolate drops.

2 Lightly grease four small individual-sized basins.

3 Divide the mixture between the basins. Cook the puddings two at a time. Put two in the microwave and cook on full power for 2-2¼ minutes. Look through the door and you will see the mixture rising in the basins. When cooked, the puddings will be just slightly moist on top. Leave in the basins for 2 minutes. Cook the other two puddings.

4 Carefully slide a knife between the puddings and the inside of the basins. Turn the basins upside down on to plates or dishes, then carefully lift them off the puddings. Serve hot with custard (see page 52) or cream.

⬛ Hi-speed Tip

If you do not have four small basins, put the mixture into 1.15-litre/ 2-pint basin and cook on full power for 2½-3½ minutes.

Peachy Delight

SERVES 4

Ingredients

100 g/4 oz ground almonds
2 trifle sponges
3-4 tablespoons raspberry
   yogurt or milk
1 (411-g/14½-oz) can peach
   halves

Chocolate sauce

1 tablespoon cornflour
4 teaspoons cocoa powder
2 tablespoons sugar

Decoration

a few glacé cherries
2 tablespoons walnut pieces

Cooking dishes

flan dish
measuring jug or basin

Method

1 Put the ground almonds in a bowl and crumble in the trifle sponges. Mix in the yogurt or milk.

2 Open the peaches and drain the syrup into a mug. Press the almond mixture into the hollows in the peach halves. Place the peaches in a flan dish, so the stuffed side is underneath. Arrange the fruit round the edge of the dish so that it cooks evenly.

3 Now make the chocolate sauce. Put the cornflour, cocoa and sugar in a heatproof measuring jug or basin. Slowly add the syrup from the peaches, stirring all the time to make the mixture smooth. Cook on full power for 2 minutes. Beat well, then cook for another 2-3 minutes, or until the sauce boils.

4 When the sauce is ready cook the peaches on full power for 3 minutes. Stir the sauce well and pour it over the peaches.

5 Chop the cherries and the walnuts, them mix them together. Sprinkle over the peaches and serve.

Gingered Apple Fool

SERVES 4

Ingredients

450 g/1 lb cooking apples
3 tablespoons water
4 tablespoons sugar
1 teaspoon ground ginger

Custard

2 tablespoons custard powder
2 tablespoons sugar
300 ml/½ pint milk

Decoration

150 ml/¼ pint double cream
4 glacé cherries

Cooking dish

2 large basins or large basin and large measuring jug

Method

1 Cut the apples into quarters. Cut out the cores and peel each piece thinly. Cut into slices. Put the apples in a large basin with the water and sugar. Add the ginger. Cover the basin and cook on full power for about 7 minutes, until really soft.

2 While the apples are cooking mix the custard powder with the sugar in a large basin or in a large measuring jug. Add a little of the milk and stir to make a smooth cream. Gradually add the rest of the milk, stirring all the time so that there are no lumps.

3 Mash the cooked apples with a potato masher until they are really smooth. Cook the custard on full power for 1 minute. Whisk well, then cook for another 2 minutes, or until the sauce boils and thickens. Whisk thoroughly. Remember to watch the custard as it cooks to make sure that it doesn't boil over the top of the basin or jug.

4 Stir the custard into the apple and leave to cool. Stir the mixture occasionally to stop a skin forming on top. Divide between four glass dishes and chill thoroughly.

5 Whip the cream until it stands in soft peaks. Fit a star nozzle in a piping bag. Spoon the cream into the bag. Pipe a large whirl on each dessert. Top each with a cherry.

⟩ Hi-speed Tip

If you have a can of ready whipped cream in the refrigerator then squirt a large swirl on each dessert.

Custard Sauce

MAKES
300 ml/½ pint

Ingredients

2 tablespoons custard
    powder
2 tablespoons sugar
300 ml/½ pint milk

Cooking dish

large basin or large
    measuring jug

Method

1 Mix the custard powder
with the sugar in a large
basin or large measuring jug.
Make sure that there is
plenty of room for the
custard to boil.

2 Gradually mix in a little of
the milk to make a smooth
paste. Add the rest of the
milk very slowly, stirring all
the time so that the sauce is
very smooth.

3 Cook on full power for 1
minute. Whisk well, then
cook for another 2 minutes
or until the custard boils.
Whisk again before serving.

Orange Custards

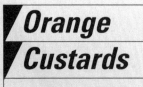

SERVES 4

Ingredients

2 small eggs
2 tablespoons sugar
grated rind of 1 orange
350 ml/12 fl oz milk

Cooking dish

large measuring jug
4 ramekins
flan dish

Method

1 Beat the eggs with the
sugar and orange rind. Heat
the milk in a measuring jug
for 3 minutes on full power.

2 Pour the milk on to the egg
mixture, beating all the time.
Divide the mixture between
four ramekins. Stand the
ramekins in a flan dish. Pour
hot water into the flan dish,
so that it surrounds the small
dishes.

3 Cook the custards on full
power for 4-5 minutes, or
until they are just set. Serve
at once, or leave to cool. Chill
the custards if you want to
serve them cold.

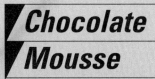

Chocolate Mousse

SERVES 4

Ingredients

3 eggs
100 g/4 oz plain chocolate
50 g/2 oz butter
grated rind of 1 orange
150 ml/¼ pint whipping
    cream
4 chocolate buttons to
    decorate

Cooking dish

large basin

Method

1 Separate the eggs before
you do anything else. If you
are not sure how to do this,
then turn to page 55 and
read the clever cook's tip.

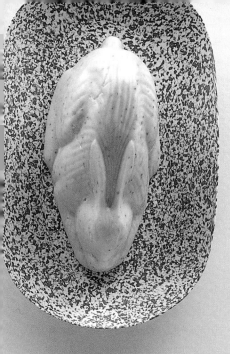

Fresh Strawberry Turnout

S E R V E S   4

Ingredients

225 g/8 oz strawberries
4 tablespoons sugar
40 g/1½ oz cornflour
350 ml/12 fl oz milk

Cooking dish

large basin

Method

1 Pick the stalks off the strawberries and rinse in cold water. Put them in a bowl and sprinkle the sugar over. Use a potato masher to crush the fruit.

2 Put the cornflour in a large basin. Add a little of the milk and stir until smooth. Slowly add the rest of the milk, stirring all the time.

3 Cook the cornflour sauce on full power for about 4 minutes or until it is boiling. Watch the sauce as it cooks to make sure that it doesn't boil over.

4 Whisk the sauce well, then stir in the crushed strawberries. Rinse out a 600-ml/1-pint mould with cold water. Pour the strawberry mixture into the mould and leave to cool. Chill well until set.

5 When set, put a plate on top of the mould, then hold both very tightly and turn the mould upside down on to the plate. Carefully lift the mould off. If the strawberry turnout is stuck, hold both the plate and mould together and give them a sharp jerk.

2 Break the chocolate into squares and put them in a large basin with the butter. Cook on full power for 2 minutes, or until the ingredients have melted.

3 While the chocolate is melting, whisk the egg whites until they stand in stiff peaks.

4 Stir the egg yolks and orange rind into the chocolate. Use a metal spoon to fold in the egg white. Do this carefully without stirring, to keep all the air in the mousse. Divide the mousse between four small dishes and chill until set. This will take several hours.

5 Whip the cream and swirl it on top of the mousses. Top each one with a chocolate button.

Orange and Raisin Cheesecake

SERVES 4 - 6

Ingredients

100 g/4 oz chocolate
   digestive biscuits
50 g/2 oz butter
2 oranges
1 tablespoon cornflour
3 tablespoons sugar
25 g/1 oz raisins
225 g/8 oz cream cheese
150 ml/¼ pint double cream
jellied orange slices to
   decorate

Cooking dishes

large basin
15-cm/6-in loose-bottomed
   cake tin

Method

1 Put the biscuits in a plastic bag. Carefully crush them with a rolling pin – make sure the bag does not burst or you will have an awful mess to clear up!

2 Put the butter in a large basin and melt it on full power for about 30 seconds. Add the biscuits and mix well. Press this mixture into the base of a 15-cm/6-in loose-bottomed cake tin. Put in the refrigerator.

3 Grate the rind from the oranges. Put it in the basin. Cut the oranges in half and squeeze all the juice from each piece. Add the cornflour and sugar to the orange rind. Gradually stir in a little of the juice to make a smooth paste. Add the rest of the juice and stir well. Add the raisins.

4 Cook on full power for 2-3 minutes, or until the sauce is boiling. Whisk well. Add the cream cheese and break it up with a wooden spoon. Beat well until the mixture is smooth.

5 Pour the cheese mixture over the biscuit base and spread it evenly. Leave to cool. Chill well.

6 To serve, slide a knife between the cheesecake and the side of the tin. Stand the tin on top of a storage jar so that the loose bottom is supported. Carefully slide the side of the tin down. Put the cheesecake on a plate.

7 Whip the cream until it stands in stiff peaks. Put a star nozzle in a piping bag. Spoon the cream into the bag and pipe it round the cheesecake. Decorate with the jellied orange slices.

Raspberry Charlotte

SERVES 4 - 6

Ingredients

1 large Swiss roll
1 egg
3 tablespoons cornflour
grated rind of 1 lemon
½ teaspoon vanilla essence
350 ml/12 fl oz milk
3 tablespoons raspberry jam
150 ml/¼ pint whipping
   cream
coloured strands to decorate

Cooking dishes

large basin
15-cm/6-in soufflé dish

Method

1 Cut the Swiss roll into slices. Carefully arrange the slices around the sides of a 15-cm/6-in soufflé dish. Make them look neat and keep any leftover slices for later.

2 Separate the egg. If you are not sure how to do this, read the clever cook's tip.

3 Mix the cornflour with the lemon rind in a large basin. Add the egg yolk and the vanilla essence. Stir well and gradually pour in the milk to make a smooth sauce. Cook on full power for 3-4 minutes, or until the sauce is boiling – it must boil. Stir in the jam.

4 Whisk the egg white until it stands in stiff peaks. Use a metal spoon to fold the white into the raspberry mixture. Just lift the raspberry mixture on the spoon and let it cover the egg white until well mixed.

5 Pour the mixture into the soufflé dish and arrange any remaining Swiss roll slices on top. Leave until cool, then put the pudding in the refrigerator for about 2 hours, or longer.

6 When you are ready to serve the pudding, carefully slide the blade of a knife between the Swiss roll and the sides of the soufflé dish. Put a plate on top and holding both very tightly, turn the dish upside down on to the plate. Lift the dish off the pudding.

7 Whip the cream until thick. Swirl the cream on the top of the pudding. Sprinkle with coloured strands and serve.

Clever Cook's Tip

To separate an egg, first get two small basins. Crack the egg round the middle. Hold it over one basin and carefully separate the shell into two. Allow the white to run into the basin but catch the yolk in one half of the shell. When all the white has run out of the other piece of shell, drop the yolk into it, hold the egg over the basin as you do this so that the white is saved. Scrape all the white from the empty shell. Put the yolk in the second basin.

A quick way is to break the egg on to a saucer. Cover the yolk with an upturned cup and drain off the white into a basin.

▌Great Cheese
▌Straws

MAKES 10

Ingredients

50 g/2 oz cheese
50 g/2 oz soft margarine
2 teaspoons made mustard
75 g/3 oz self-raising flour
1 teaspoon snipped chives
2 tablespoons sesame seeds
¼ teaspoon paprika

Cooking dish

large flan dish

Method

1 Grate the cheese, then put it in a bowl with the margarine and mustard. Beat well, using a wooden spoon, until really creamy and well combined.

2 Add the flour and chives and stir to form a firm mixture. Use your fingers to press the mixture into a ball. Lightly flour the work surface and knead the mixture for a few seconds until smooth.

3 Roll the dough into one long piece, then cut it into ten slices. Roll the slices into thin straws, measuring about 15 cm/6 in each. Mix the sesame seeds and paprika on a plate, then roll the straws in this mixture to coat them completely.

4 Lay five straws as far apart as possible in a large flan dish. Cook on full power for 3-3½ minutes. The straws will rise and spread out a bit as they cook.

5 Leave the straws on the dish for a minute, then use a long palette knife or fish slice to lift them off. Put them on a wire rack to cool. Cook the other five straws in the same way.

◀ Clever Cook's Tip

These cheese straws taste great with a dip. Try serving them with a bowl of cottage cheese and chives or any favourite dip.

Cocoa Crisps

MAKES 16

Ingredients

75 g/3 oz butter
3 tablespoons jelly
 marmalade
100 g/4 oz Cocoa Pops
50 g/2 oz chopped toasted
 hazelnuts
50 g/2 oz raisins

Cooking dish

large bowl or casserole dish

Method

1 Put the butter and jelly marmalade in a large bowl or casserole dish. Cook on full power for 1-1½ minutes, or until melted.

2 Add the Cocoa Pops, nuts and raisins and mix really well. Set the mixture aside until the butter and marmalade get sticky and begin to set.

3 Get ready 16 paper cake cases, putting them in bun tins or on a tray.

4 Stir the mixture well and use a teaspoon to divide it between the paper cases. Chill until firm.

Coconut Pyramids

MAKES 10

Ingredients

1 egg white
2 tablespoons icing sugar
100 g/4 oz desiccated
 coconut
3 glacé cherries

Cooking dish

large flat plate or flan dish

Method

1 In a large basin, whisk the egg white until it is frothy. Add the icing sugar and whisk until very stiff.

2 Add the desiccated coconut to the egg and stir it in to make a stiff mixture.

3 Wet your hands to prevent the mixture from sticking to them and shape large teaspoonfuls of the mixture into small pyramids, pressing them together really well.

4 Cut the cherries into quarters. Place a piece of cherry on each coconut pyramid, pressing it on firmly.

5 Place five coconut pyramids as far apart as possible round the edge of a large flat plate or flan dish. Cook on full power for 1½ minutes, or until firm. Leave the pyramids on the plate for 2 minutes, then put them on a wire rack to cool. Cook the other five in the same way.

Iced Honey Buns

MAKES 12

Ingredients

50 g/2 oz soft margarine
25 g/1 oz caster sugar
2 tablespoons clear honey
50 g/2 oz self-raising flour
1 egg

Icing

100 g/4 oz icing sugar
1 tablespoon lemon juice
6 glacé cherries to decorate

Cooking dish

large plate
24 paper cake cases

Method

1 Put the margarine, sugar, honey, flour and egg in a bowl. Use a wooden spoon to beat all the ingredients together until very creamy and pale.

2 Put four double-thick paper cake cases on a plate. Put another eight double cases to one side. Use a teaspoon to divide the cake mixture between all 12 cake cases.

3 Cook the four cakes on the plate using full power for 1-1¼ minutes, or until risen and just slightly moist on top. Transfer the cakes to a wire rack to cool. Cook the remaining cakes four at a time in the same way.

4 To make the icing, sift the icing sugar into a basin. Add the lemon juice and beat well until smooth. Cut the cherries in half.

5 When the cakes are completely cold, spread a little icing on top of each one. Top each with a piece of cherry and leave until set.

Coconut Buns

MAKES 12

Ingredients

50 g/2 oz soft margarine
50 g/2 oz caster sugar
50 g/2 oz self-raising flour
25 g/1 oz desiccated coconut
1 egg
2 tablespoons milk

Decoration

3 tablespoons red jam
4 tablespoons desiccated
   coconut

Cooking dishes

large plate
24 paper cake cases
small basin

Method

1 Put the margarine, sugar, flour, coconut, egg and milk in a bowl. Use a wooden spoon to beat the ingredients together until very soft and pale.

2 Get ready 12 double thick paper cake cases and put four on a large plate.

3 Use a teaspoon to divide the cake mixture between the paper cases.

58

4 Cook the four cakes on the plate using full power for 1-1¼ minutes, or until the mixture has risen but is still slightly moist on top. Lift them on to a wire rack to cool. Cook the remaining cakes, four at a time, in the same way.

5 To make the decoration, put the jam in a small basin and cook on full power for about 30 seconds to warm it. Spread the jam over the top of the cakes and sprinkle with a little coconut.

Chocolate Ring Cake

SERVES 6

Ingredients

50 g/2 oz soft margarine
50 g/2 oz caster sugar
50 g/2 oz self-raising flour
2 tablespoons cocoa powder
1 egg
2 tablespoons milk

Icing

1 tablespoon cocoa powder
knob of butter
2 tablespoons water
100 g/4 oz icing sugar

Decoration

piece of angelica
walnut halves

Cooking dish

900-ml/1½-pint ring dish
large basin

Method

1 Put the margarine, sugar, flour, cocoa powder, egg and milk in a bowl. Use a wooden spoon to beat all the ingredients together until very soft and creamy.

2 Grease a 900-ml/1½-pint ring dish with a little oil. Put the mixture into the dish, spreading it evenly in the base. It will need plenty of room to rise during cooking.

3 Cook on full power for about 2½ minutes. Watch the cake as it cooks. It will rise and should be just slightly moist on top when it is done.

4 Leave the cake in the dish for 4-5 minutes, then turn it out on to a wire rack to cool.

5 To make the icing, put the cocoa powder, butter and water in a large basin and cook on full power for 30 seconds, until the butter melts. Sift the icing sugar into the basin and beat well until smooth. Spoon the icing over the cooled cake, allowing it to run down the sides.

6 Cut strips of angelica into small leaves. Put walnut halves and angelica leaves round the top of the cake and leave the icing to set.

Flapjack Cups

Ingredients

2 tablespoons crunchy
 peanut butter
3 tablespoons thick honey
50 g/2 oz butter
125 g/5 oz muesli

Cooking dish

large basin
large plate
16 paper cake cases

Method

1 Put the peanut butter,
honey and butter in a large
basin and cook on full power
for 1 minute, or until melted.

2 Add the muesli and mix
well. Get ready eight double-
thick paper cake cases. Use a
teaspoon to divide the
mixture between the cases,
pressing it down firmly.

3 Put four on a large plate
and cook on full power for
about 1 minute, until the
mixture is sizzling and
cooked.

4 Lift the four cooked
flapjack cups on to a wire
rack to cool and cook the
other four in the same way.

Muesli Biscuits

MAKES 12

Ingredients

50 g/2 oz margarine
2 tablespoons dark soft
 brown sugar
100 g/4 oz muesli
50 g/2 oz self-raising flour
1 tablespoon orange juice

Cooking dish

large flan dish

Method

1 Put the margarine and
sugar in a bowl. Use a
wooden spoon to cream the
ingredients together until
really soft and pale.

2 Stir in the muesli, flour and
orange juice to make a firm
mixture.

3 Take pieces of the mixture
about the size of walnuts.
Flour your fingers and roll
the mixture into balls. You
should make 12 balls.

4 Place six of the balls as far
apart as possible round
the edge of a large flan dish.
Use a fork to flatten the
biscuits. Cook on full power
for 2-2½ minutes, or until the
biscuits are sizzling and firm.
Leave on the dish for 3-4
minutes, then use a flat
palette knife to lift the
biscuits on to a wire rack.

5 Cook the remaining six
biscuits in the same way.

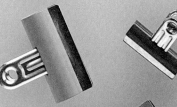

Peanut Shorties

MAKES 10

Ingredients

50 g/2 oz soft margarine
2 tablespoons dark soft
  brown sugar
2 tablespoons crunchy
  peanut butter
100 g/4 oz self-raising flour
1 tablespoon water

Cooking dish

flan dish

Method

1 Grease a flan dish with a
little cooking oil. Put the
margarine, sugar and peanut
butter in a bowl. Use a
wooden spoon to cream the
ingredients together until
really soft.

2 Stir in the flour and the
water to make a stiff dough.
Take pieces of the mixture,
about the size of a walnut.
Lightly flour your fingers and
roll each piece of dough into
a ball. You should make ten
balls. Place them as far apart
as possible round the edge
of the flan dish.

3 Use a large fork to flatten
the cookies. Cook on full
power for 1½-2 minutes. The
cookies will rise and spread a
little. When cooked they
should be just firm on top.
Leave for 3-4 minutes, then
use a palette knife to lift them
on to a wire rack.

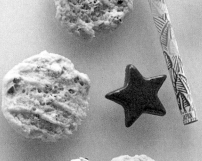

Choc-chip Cookies

MAKES 12

Ingredients

50 g/2 oz soft margarine
1 teaspoon vanilla essence
50 g/2 oz caster sugar
2 tablespoons toasted
  chopped hazelnuts
100 g/4 oz self-raising flour
25 g/1 oz chocolate drops for
  cooking
1 tablespoon water

Cooking dish

large flan dish

Method

1 Put the margarine, vanilla
essence and sugar in a bowl.
Use a wooden spoon to
cream the ingredients
together until pale and soft.

2 Stir in the nuts, flour,
chocolate drops and water to
make a stiff mixture. Take
pieces of the mixture about
the size of walnuts. Lightly
flour your hands and shape
each portion of the mixture
into a ball. You should make
12 balls.

3 Place the balls as far apart
as possible round the edge
of a large flan dish. Use a
large fork to press them flat.
Cook on full power for 2
minutes, or until the mixture
is firm. Leave on the dish for
3-4 minutes, then use a flat
palette knife to lift them on to
a wire rack to cool.

SWEET TREATS

Truffles

MAKES 24

Ingredients

100 g/4 oz plain chocolate
2 tablespoons orange juice
1 tablespoon raspberry jam
225 g/8 oz plain cake
chocolate vermicelli for
    coating

Cooking dish

large basin

Method

1 Break the chocolate into squares and place them in a large basin with the orange juice and jam. Cook on full power for 1½ minutes, or until the chocolate has melted.

2 Break the cake into fine crumbs and add to the melted mixture. Stir well to combine the ingredients.

3 Shape the mixture into small balls and roll them in the chocolate vermicelli. Place on a plate or dish and chill until firm.

Chocolate Banana Crunchies

MAKES ABOUT 16

Ingredients

225 g/8 oz plain chocolate
2 firm bananas
75 g/3 oz desiccated coconut

Cooking dish

large basin

Method

1 Break the chocolate into squares and place them in a large basin. Melt the chocolate on medium power for 2 minutes. Stir well, then cook on medium power for a further 2 minutes, or until the chocolate has melted completely.

2 Peel the bananas and cut them into chunks. Put the coconut in a pudding bowl. Lay a piece of greaseproof paper on a flat board. Stick a fork into a chunk of banana, then dip it into the chocolate to coat it completely. Hold it over the basin for a few seconds to let any excess chocolate drip off. Use the point of a knife to push the banana off the fork on to the coconut in the dish. Sprinkle coconut over the top of the chocolate.

3 Use a spoon and fork to lift the chocolate-coated banana out of the coconut. Place it on the greaseproof paper and leave to set. Dip and coat all the chunks of banana, then put the board in a cool place until the chocolate has hardened.

3 Cook on full power for about 7 minutes, stirring once after 5 minutes. The mixture should boil rapidly and when cooked it should be very buttery and thick. Break the chocolate into squares.

4 Use oven gloves to lift the dish from the oven. Using a wooden spoon, beat well until creamy. Add the chocolate and stir until dissolved. Beat well until thick and creamy.

5 Turn the mixture into the greased tin and spread it evenly. Leave until cold, then chill lightly. Cut into squares.

Easy Fudge

*MAKES ABOUT
40 PIECES*

Ingredients

1 (400-g/14.1-oz) can
  sweetened condensed
  milk
100 g/4 oz butter
225-g/8-oz plain chocolate

Cooking dish

large casserole dish or
  mixing bowl

Method

1 Lightly grease a 18-cm/7-in square tin (you can use a 20-cm/8-in round sandwich tin if you don't have a square one).

2 Scrape all the condensed milk into a large casserole dish or a mixing bowl which can go in the microwave. Make sure that there is plenty of room for it to boil. Add the butter.

Peanut Brittle

*MAKES
1 20-cm/8-in round*

Ingredients

225 g/8 oz sugar
8 tablespoons water
100 g/4 oz salted peanuts
25 g/1 oz butter
¼ teaspoon bicarbonate of
  soda

Cooking dish

large soufflé dish or
  casserole dish

Method

1 Put the sugar into a large soufflé dish or casserole dish. Add the water and stir well. There should be plenty of room for the mixture to boil up as it cooks. Cook on full power for 10 minutes.

2 Use oven gloves to remove the dish from the oven. Stir the syrup well, pushing any sugar down off the sides of the dish. Cook on full power for another 5-7 minutes. Watch the mixture carefully. It will begin to turn brown (caramelise) – you must open the oven door when it is a pale golden colour. It will carry on cooking after it is removed from the oven and darken slightly.

3 The dish is *very* hot. Have a pan stand or table mat ready to put the dish on. Lift it with oven gloves. Taking care, add the nuts, butter and bicarbonate of soda all at once. Stir with a wooden spoon.

4 Lightly grease a sandwich tin (about 20-cm/8-in across). Pour the mixture into the tin, scraping all the caramel from the dish. Leave until cold and set hard. Break up the brittle with a steak mallet or rolling pin. Store in an airtight container.

INDEX